A collection of the occasions on which God has revealed Himself to her through both voice and feeling, Patricia Roedema's *A Tribute to Spirit* captures the way in which her unbreakable faith has successfully guided her from times of pain and suffering to times of peace and happiness.

– Stephanie Peterson, author of the *Welcome to Keystone* Series

D1304261

To
Michelle Clark
Blessing and peace
Patricia Roedema

12-7-19

A TRIBUTE TO SPIRIT

A TRIBUTE TO SPIRIT

BY

PATRICIA ROEDEMA

A TRIBUTE TO SPIRIT

ISBN: 9781798496404

Edited by Stephanie J. Beavers Communications
www.StephanieJBeavers.com
610–247–9494

Cover design by Biddle Design
www.BiddleDesign.com

Dedication

To my devoted and beloved husband – my fire, my music. Our three wonderful children, their loving spouses, and our beautiful grandchildren are gently woven into the golden tapestry of this work.

Preface

As a young woman I suffered from back pain and migraine headaches. A very dear friend, Kay Lennon, heard about Edgar Cayce, a psychic who suggested cures with natural remedies for every type of ailment. The two of us took off for our Monroe town library where we found Cayce's book *A Search for God*. The book contained the name, address, and phone number of a woman nearby who held Edgar Cayce study group meetings in her home. I can recall the anticipation and exhilaration I felt at that first meeting. I was home.

I was especially drawn to one of the members, Peg Haraske, who became my teacher and guide. The works of world religions, universal truth, and spiritual consciousness were my daily bread. April 5, 1970, cosmic consciousness was bestowed on me, seeming to peak in enlightenment January 13, 1972. Spiritual life is not contained in mortal time. It flows like ocean waves embracing the shore – homecoming. My teacher's advice was to tell no one of these experiences and to record all for the time when they would be of value.

Open your heart to this message. Read it slowly. Allow it to speak to you.

Clarification of Terms

Meditation: Opening mind and heart with the intent and sole purpose to communion with God. Meditation sessions could occur on different days or multiple times in a single day.

Night Notes: Recordings of words or experiences arising from my subconscious mind when awakened from a deep sleep. Night notes had to be recorded as clearly as possible at the time or they would have been forgotten.

Processing: I use this word to refer to the activity between the subconscious and conscious mind when sensation, emotion, message, or vision comes up. Through understanding, forgiving, and embracing, we own it, we relive it, we are it. We allow error to lead to truth.

Reiki: Healing energy work similar to New Testament laying on of hands.

Revelation: What is revealed to me by God. Webster's Dictionary: revealed by God to man; an act of communicating or revealing divine truth; an act of revealing to vision or making known.

Throughout the book random names appear. Those that are not identified are voices of a distant past, long forgotten, that speak to me; friends on earth and in heaven.

1970

April 5

I was sitting on the couch. Alone. Ed, Donna (age 7), and Doug (age 5) were at church and Tom (age 10 months) was sleeping. I was reading *Everyman's Search* by Rebecca Beard. The words of the book lifted off the page in front of me – three dimensionally. I felt the words reach me. I had read and heard them before but, in that second, I finally understood them. This understanding was accompanied by a feeling of being above my physical self and detached from it. I felt deeply aware of a greater power surging through me. I was drifting along on what felt like a wave, a current. I felt both very much a part of the entire whole, while also above all things earthly.

I felt full of love. In fact, never had I felt so loving. I saw every thing and every body with other eyes – the eyes of the spirit. I had no hunger. I wanted nothing. Nothing was impossible. Everything was easy. I could do anything that was required of me, yet not be touched by it. No longer was I afraid to accept "the way" – the way of Spirit, of God. I *knew* God would guide me and supply my every need. I was no longer afraid of anyone's company or the influence they might have over me. Nothing could touch me. I knew I could attain that state forever. It's always here – we just need to allow it to come. I gave thanks to Peg Harakse for her unfailing support and help. I gave thanks for everything.

This state of Consciousness lasted through Thursday, April 9, when I was stricken with a headache and got upset at Doug (unjustly). I longed to get back to that state, that place, but soon realized I could not want that. I needed to get back to the moment and be grateful for it.

While in meditation, I heard from within, "Peace I give you, not as the world gives, give I unto you." I heard and felt the words. The next day it came.

April 10

Today was Doug's birthday. Donna was home with a sore throat, and she and Doug were watching TV. Thomas was sleeping. I meditated and was aware of a faint, fragrant Presence, a sweet, sweet odor no mortal mind can describe – a taste of Heaven, Lord God Himself. I somehow knew that if I breathed deeply, the scent would disappear. Instinctively, I also wanted to breathe deeply to take more of it in, but altered spiritual states are not humanly controllable. They happen of their own. We do nothing. We are witness to Spirit. The scent remained with me throughout the meditation. I was sitting on the couch staring out the window and contemplating. All of a sudden, I was looking through rose–colored glasses. Gray clouds turned pink, then blue, then green and all colors of the rainbow as they passed before me. Then showers of rays of light descended on me.

 Unlike my first experience where I felt above all things earthly, this time I did not. I was, however, aware of a power working through me, knowing I was not doing anything; the power was doing it all.

May 10

The family was in church. Thomas was napping and I was outside, reading *Cosmic Consciousness*.[1] I set the book down and went inside to meditate. I became aware of a pulsing light on my forehead and felt the urge to go to the window. I looked at the sky, which became deep blue and was filled with stars. A spot of bright light in the center of the sky came to me. The light was from Heaven and *I* became bright. The light was from *within* me. I felt God within. I *knew* God within. I experienced God within. The entire area surrounding me was white. Previously, His blessings had been bestowed upon me from without, or so I thought. I sat for twenty minutes in that awareness. If Tom hadn't needed me, I could have remained in that place forever. It is eternity.

May 13

I sat on my bed and looked out the window. I gave thanks to God. I became blinded by, and emerged into, oneness. The objects all around me disappeared.

July 8

Pastor Schwartz visited. Throughout our conversation, I was emotionally detached and not the one who spoke. Rather, a voice spoke through me. When I turned off the lights to go to bed, I saw a bright light in the middle of my forehead. It had been there all evening, but I only became aware of it in the dark. The light was about the size of a quarter, and I saw it whether my eyes were

---

[1] *Cosmic Consciousness: A Study in the Evolution of the Human Mind*. Originally written in 1901 by Canadian psychiatrist Richard Maurice Bucke.

open or closed. During my conversation with Pastor, I saw pinpoints of brilliant white light again and again.

July 10

Meditation: Over the past few days, I felt myself being drawn inward, as if all my extremities were being pulled in. This time, I felt and saw milk – sweet, sweet milk – being poured into my mouth. I then felt enveloped by *something*. I was breathless. In my mind, a voice asked, "Are you afraid?" I thought, "Yes. I've never been here before." The voice then said, "Get used to it. You will be many times."

1971

March 18

Meditation: I felt drawn inward, filled by a breath. I wondered what was happening. In a flash, I saw myself dressed in a white satin gown. I was being joined to a spirit form, not human. This image appeared in a corner of my mind. A voice said, "I can't stay, but I will be here when you need me."

1972

January 13

I had a realization of freedom from the need to know "how" to be a perfect mother to my children, as I was always hesitating as to how much attention to give them, more freedom or less. Ed traveled with his work for long periods of time. I felt insecure without his support. I knew I was humanly faulty and wanted to know how I could please God. I wrote a letter to my spiritual mentor, Peg Haraske. Deep down, I knew the letter was really to myself, as I was asking for the missing link. I was receiving no guidance and I still did not know what to do with my children. I read the letter over, at which time everything became clear. I had to act, but do so *knowing* it was God acting through me. I didn't need to stop and ask God, but instead have faith that God would do what was needed. I would dedicate myself anew each day, then do what seemed to need doing at the time. God will show me when I need correction. The "missing link" is that continuation, the letting–matters–flow–through without hesitation or doubt. This is love, and I am sending it back to God. This is our freedom – actions that fall from us because they are dedicated through, and in, love. These actions aren't ours any more than our children are ours. Suddenly, it was clear! The realization of freedom and newness to all things every day. As I sit here today, I am still uncertain what to do, but I trust God acts through me and we will continue that way forever. Ours is only to love God – not to question or ask, but to assume it.

After feeling like I am hanging between two worlds of *what is* and *what seems to be*, and holding onto that IS when I don't feel It, It, It, but hope for and claim It, It becomes so.

Meditation: Pulsing crown chakra[2] – I felt drawn up and out of body. I was gone for a half hour, though it seemed like only a few

---

[2] According to ancient cultures, within us are seven centers of energy: the chakras. The chakras start at the base of the spine (the root chakra) and move to the top of the head (the crown chakra). Body, mind, and spirit receive the proper amount of energy when we are healthy and balanced. Our health suffers if a chakra is too open or too closed, or spinning too quickly or too slowly. The color associated with the root chakra, which connects our energy with Earth, is red. The color associated with the crown chakra, which is pure

seconds. In a corner of my mind, I saw myself as a spirit bride with a groom. I heard the words, "The fusion has been made."

Meditation: I was immediately taken deep within in awareness. There was much talking, of which nothing was sensible or remembered. Several people were with me. I felt profoundly centered and still. Time was not. When I came to and opened my eyes, I stood up, as if in a dream. I felt I was floating, though not physically. I went to the kitchen counter and was directed to place my hand on it. My hand went through the top and into the counter. It, or rather I, was not solid. However, I functioned clearly, prepared meals, and cared for my family as a physical being. I remained in this state of consciousness for fifteen days.

February 3

A friend of mine, Mary Solliday, related a report in *The Wall Street Journal* about intelligence in plant life, fruits, and other non–human living things. Quietly, deeply, a realization came: I beheld a reverence for all things.

Everything now speaks to me and I feel communication with it. I've been seeing color around people and things in dreams. This seems like the vibration and being of each thing or person as it takes hold, becoming sure. I feel surrounded by life and by godliness in all forms.

I asked for moderation in my housework and daily duties. I felt compelled, stressed, to address my duties. My intent and desire is to be in harmony in thought and action. God did it for me again.

---

consciousness energy, is violet or white. Source:
https://blog.mindvalley.com/7–chakras/?utm_source=google_blog.

Now each thing is holy in itself and my actions with it have feeling. God answers our call.

1973

September 27

A realization: We must give up God for God's sake! Give up practicing God, the lessons, the exercise – everything must go. As long as we think we need lessons, we will get them. God is perfect. He doesn't teach or instruct; He simply *is*. Pure being. We are the Light now. It is within us.

Practicing God is as far from God as everything. God is not a thing. All that is *not* must be given up. This dynamic is subtle, because one feels so good in the work one is doing. Positive versus negative. It must be an inner revelation. One is no higher or closer to God than the other. God encompasses all. Good is better than evil. This is still the mortal mind working. From now on, it's God's work. He is doing the work and needs no practice or teaching. I claim I am perfect – the perfect light! Oh, yes!

I must stop talking about it the same way negative thoughts are given up. This can be a worse state than the first because it looks good and feels good. (Look what I am doing.) I caught a glimpse of this earlier, then lost it when I was instructing others – even without the intention to teach! The greatest teacher is silence.

The *presence* transforms all things, permeates all things, uplifts all things – in essence, the presence brings all to higher consciousness. The presence comes from within and is common with all and is where it happens.

I saw myself hanging on the edge of a cliff, peeking over and simply glorifying the *truth*. Such beauty and happiness now, but there is more to come – unspeakable splendor words cannot express.

Meditation: There is much light: circles of light. Depth of light. A being descended into the depth and said, "Stand forth, Beloved." The being then rose. I watched myself the entire night as I went in and out of consciousness. I was given other signs I was not to write down. I knew it was part of me as I needed it, not to be used for ego in any way.

1978

We moved to Mansfield, Ohio, when Ed accepted a position with Tappan. This is a Bible belt. Art Crawford, minister at Riverside Bible Church in Columbus, taught the Bible on foundations of Greek and Hebrew. This shed new light and understanding on the Bible, falling in line with Truth of all ages. Thank you, Art, for your faithful service. We lived in Mansfield for ten years.

1985

July 8, Ohio

Reaching consciousness is much like breaking the sound barrier and keeping yourself together. You then experience freedom. That day, I was picking berries and a clear awareness came that involved the freedom I felt with my daughter, Donna, getting married. I had wondered at that realization of freedom, as I had no conflict with her and knew only love for my daughter. Something was completed, but I knew not what. Clarity now came that Donna had a problem with her father and me. She was subconsciously jealous of our relationship. Whatever was being worked out, we are both free of it.

July 9

Dream: It was someone's wedding. My sister Evelyn's house was located under the church, in the basement. At the last minute, my daughter, Donna, asked to wear my pink dress. I let her have it, but then had no dress of my own. I looked for a dress of Evie's but was unable to find it and I didn't want to bother her, as she was busy with guests. I was also unable to find stockings, so I went without. Evie came in and gave me a dress.

I'm being prepared for the wedding feast. I *know* God is guiding me in all areas of my life for this purpose. Out of sight, the work is going on. As above, so below. When the bride is ready, conscious and subconscious join. As one, working together. My spiritual eye and ear became sharp and clear, seeing and listening clearly.

1987

December

Ed was invited by his brother–in–law to join him in his business in Lancaster, Pennsylvania, and we moved to nearby Lebanon. I trained for six years in Gestalt Pastoral Care[3], studied therapeutic massage and attained a master's degree in Usui Shiki Ryoho, a system of Reiki natural healing.

---

[3] Gestalt therapy is a wholistic approach to healing.

1997

January 6

Night vision: I saw an angel constellation low in the sky and went to it. Rays poured down on a man, a woman, and a child. I stepped in front of them and they stepped aside. I said, "I will get up every morning at this time to be with my angel."

March 1

I received initiation into first degree Reiki. While receiving Reiki, I felt great sadness. Ed was not doing his spiritual work. I felt I had failed him, then recognized the lie. His work is his responsibility, not mine. But I took on his failure. I separate myself from what I believe is his failure.

My father died when I was four. As I grew, I felt ashamed of being without a father. Through therapy, it became clear that I carried my mother's shame, for she was born out of wedlock and never knew her father.

March 2

Meditation: Anne and Anna came in. They were my mother's mother and grandmother, respectively. Both died before I was born, so I didn't know them and never felt connected to them. They came into my space to be acknowledged and released. I expressed sorrow for the shame they both carried while alive – for the pain and confusion they experienced, especially the sexual abuse.[4] I cried. I spoke to them of forgiveness, released them from the bondage of shame. I then blessed them and sent them on. I cut

---

[4] Sexual abuse was revealed in my mother's story.

connections between them and all future generations in our family line. I also released Grandpa and Daddy. I forgave them both and sent them on with blessings.

I thanked them all for my heritage – my home of origin, my connection with the land and animals, my healthy life – their hard work secured all this for me. They needed the release. Grandmother and daughter were dancing, experiencing freedom, lightness, and joy. I am honored to be part of it all.

August 2

Processing (vision) 3:00 a.m.: I saw a water pipe coming out of the ground near the outhouse at my childhood home. I also saw myself fall into a pigpen. I was two or three years old and wearing a brand new blue snowsuit. My mother said, "We'll never get the dirt out." I was not attracted to the color blue.

At eight years of age, a calf stepped on my left foot as I held her rope for a photo. The picture that came out was of me screaming in agony. Whenever I saw that picture, I felt ashamed and thought, "I didn't do it right. I ruined the picture." Now, at age 58, I realize my left foot has been hurting for a year. The pain resembled that of my toes being split the way a hoof is split.

Night notes: "To never look at again." Then I hear, "Who?" My mother's voice says, "I forget. It's too hard to remember." I see someone pulling down a shade. When I was a child, the shades were always half drawn.

Now awake, I remembered my aunt's house where I spent preschool days while Mother was at work. The living room was dark, the shades were drawn. At Christmas, I was allowed to go into the living room to see the tree, but then get right out. Cousin Gladys had shiny jewelry and soft sweaters and all sorts of things. I wanted to touch them all but was told not to. I longed just to feel them, nothing more. I realized how I picked up and handled things in stores. I didn't want to buy them, just feel them.

Night notes: "If you ever had it, you'd never know." Mrs. Wilkinson, my fourth- and fifth-grade teacher talked about illness and disease. "Draper never had it so Draper never knew." Draper was the name of my high school. "Big stomach – from having children." That referred to Aunt Ann. I felt pain in the left side of my stomach, under the rib and down. I felt other pains that were sharp like pins, like straw or hay pricking me. My face felt itchy. "It was the first time I ever met him" (Mother's voice). I drew my hand over my forehead and eyes as if I were just waking up. The scene I see, a memory from my childhood, is of a cow giving birth. The cow needed help, as the calf's rear was coming out first. I heard the cow moo and cry in pain. I heard and felt it. Voice said, "It's nobody's business." Mother said, "No, we don't have that." Night words ended.

Gestalt therapy session with Gestalt pastoral care minister Rhoda Glick: In Gestalt, truth is revealed. To never look at again. I was at my father's graveside. Jesus opened his casket. I was stunned, unable to move, as I looked at my dad. I had wanted to look in the coffin at the time of my father's burial because I could not believe he was in there. Mother said I would never see him again. I couldn't believe that either. I started laughing. "You said I'd never see him again, but I did!" What truth did I learn? *Never* does not exist and life is forever.

Fear and disease are lies. This was a *never* lock involved in both illness and lies, existing in several chains which fell apart in the light of truth having no energy of its own.

The cow's birth hid in my subconscious and played out in the emotionally and physically painful birth of my daughter.

"It was the first time I ever met him" (Mother's voice). I drew my hand across my eyes and my forehead several times. I experienced this in the womb. I knew Mother was lying. "How can that be?" I knew the truth from the womb. A window shade was being pulled, though I did not observe it directly. Mother was having intercourse with a man, I don't know who. I knew she was a liar before I was born. I had carried her lies and her shit all these years and never confronted her. I didn't want to believe it. I was afraid she'd leave me if she realized that I knew. I felt angry at taking all her shit and lies. And, it made me a liar too – for not telling and seeing the truth!

I did not want any more of this crap. I told Mother I knew all about her lies. I put the lies and the pain in a gray bag, but I did not want to give this load to Mother. I was too fearful. I asked Jesus in and gave Him the bag. He set the load behind him on the ground and said, "Get thee behind me, Satan." At that point, the therapist made a remark about needing to know who I was. I was confused at that, but continued. Jesus put his hand to my mother's and my shoulders. I didn't know what he was doing, and even wondered how he could possibly reconcile us. I saw he was separating us. He dislodged the energy that had bound us together – the lies and the pain – and I was thrilled by the experience. It was a miracle. Awesome.

I looked into my mother's eyes as if for the first time. It was a moment of truth. I felt exhilarated, free – I was my own person. I asked for energy to be directed to Mother's knee. It had been painful a long time. Jesus took care of my request in the very moment I made it. Mother can heal now. Jesus set us free. I was filled with lightness and life. It was wonderful! I praised God over and over for his life and his goodness.

Rhoda prayed for my stomach to be free of its pain (all the pain and lies I held in) and to be whole – to be free to support itself, as it is created to, and to hold itself in a healthy place. I thanked the doctor who had pressed on it after giving birth – he did what he had to do.

Processing 11:30 p.m. – 3 a.m.: The bedsheet tickled my feet and legs. I felt the need to move. It was driving me crazy. I scratched my left foot, then felt a tingling sensation from my feet up the outside of both legs. I became aware of a gas or air being released into my abdomen. I heard the harsh sound it made as it exploded.

Male voice: "I didn't know you knew French."

Female voice: "Oh, I'm sorry. I'm sorry." I was feeling sensation in a tooth, in a dentist's chair having work done.

My voice (from deep within): "My fear is that I won't be able to find what I'm looking for."

Female voice: "He must come home at night."

Female voice: "Takes a lot of pressure to make him do that."

An emphatic, emotional female voice said: "He *must* do that!"

16

I was aware of my own fast, heavy breathing. I felt fear and anticipated pain.

Male voice: "That's the locks. We can't get at them."

Male voice in a dialect: "Is this returning? What am I doing?"

I felt a heavy sensation in my stomach. "There is nothing. Being enthusiastic again." My right eye pulses.

Female voice: "The end of that beautiful, glorious chain. The link between God and man."

Pulse in root chakra – I experienced enthusiasm, joy.

Female voice: "Will always feel the same way you do." I felt the tingling of the sympathy gland in my fanny. "You're hitting with my touches." I must touch sensations in my body (they call for my attention).

A thought came. Tomatoes are an acid and can cause itching.

Female voice: "I don't come a lot. You're never home."

I saw Aunt Ann's big stomach. Mom Roedema's (my mother–in–law) voice: "I looked for you."

Aware of my heart beating faster. I was at Aunt Ann's funeral, and said, "I never went to visit you. I'm sorry." I felt grief and emotion. My voice held compassion. I had been lying on my left side and shifted my knee slightly. At that movement, a change occurred in my body consciousness. So, a shift of the body's position results in a change to the body's consciousness.

My awareness voice: "Might as well get rid of the potatoes tonight."

Female voice: "Good. I love potatoes."

I was lying on my back, aware of my beating heart.

Scene and sound: A child scolding another child. Me, perhaps?

"You mustn't knock it. Gently, gently." I heard these words spoken with much emotion and yelling.

My awareness voice: "When you get to the basic thought, you don't have to remember. You are to act."

My cousin Pearl's voice: "More fun in this little factory."

Female voice: "Wonderful girl!" The voice was full of enthusiasm, joy, praise.

My awareness voice: "Of course, I don't remember ever asking for it."

I became aware of going into sleep. I was aware of my heart. Was I asleep? Was I dead?

My awareness voice: "Stay there." The atmosphere was fuzzy. My vision hazy. "No fear."

End for the night.[5]

---

[5] Gestalt healing work brings up issues from the subconscious needing the light of truth.

August 4

Night processing: I was back in Dr. Chauvin's (the dentist) chair.
He worked on my right eye tooth where the gum was inflamed.
Jesus entered and removed the clamp. The clamp had caused me a
lot of pain while the dentist filled my tooth. But Jesus's hand in
my mouth healed the gum and also the trauma of a previous
dentist extracting an abscessed tooth. "Thank you, my Lord and
Savior." Then Jesus comforted me. I put my head on his shoulder.
Back in the dentist chair, Jesus held my head in his hands and had
me open my mouth. He put spit on his fingers and wiped my lips
which were cracked at the corners from being held open for so
long. I felt no pain. Jesus healed me. Thank you, my Lord.

I am at Aunt Ann's house. I went into the living room with her to
look at the Christmas tree. I touched all the gifts. Jesus said, "This
isn't what Christmas is about, these things. It's my birth. I am the
gift." I felt satisfied. I thanked Aunt Ann for caring for me and
keeping me all those years. I felt great sorrow at not visiting her
even once after I grew up. I asked God's blessing on her, wherever
she is.

August 5

Night processing/night notes: The lock

I saw a brass lock sticking out of a door, so the door is open to the
lock on tickling. I couldn't move. I couldn't get away. I was being
sat on and held down by my big brother. I was aware of a sweet
odor, a fragrant presence. A voice said, "Might say the air tickles
her fanny." The dentist gave me laughing gas. Ed's breathing on

me or my own breath on me disturbs me at night. My whole body wants to scream. I leave it.

I am in water – at Six Mile Run Reservoir. I was five years old and I drowned. I saw myself rise to the top. My sister Evelyn saved me. "So, shall I call him?" (the words came from within). "I don't know. Why are you pressing me?" I felt pain on the back left side of my head. I did my own work – Jesus, be with me. I looked over my processing notes. I see the lock. The door is open so I can go in and get what I am looking for, as it is available.

September 1, Labor Day

I experienced sunrise on the beach at Sacandaga Reservoir. I saw red and green, with an elongated center, a guide. A silver color rose from the water.

Night experience: I heard a scream – it was my own scream. I screamed. Then I saw Grandpa's death. I was by Mother's side. She was feeding Grandpa noodle soup. The noodles were in his mouth. She then took them out by hand, speaking sweetly and sadly as she did so. I saw his spirit leave. I knew – felt – that experience within me. I was three at the time. I took a step back, out of that space and asked, "Where do I go from here? What do I do with this?" Realized I do nothing – it's a gift.

October 29

Night note: "Throw me a rope." Someone was drowning in pain.

When I visited my mother, she was tied up in knots. Her neck and back were tight – as hard as concrete. I worked on her feet and gave her a massage and Reiki on her knee. "What can I do for her,

Lord? She's so sad and fearful." Mother shared her pain: Jeff (her grandson) wants land; no matter what she does, someone will not love her; Evelyn (my sister) has not been real with her. We prayed and read the Bible for her to receive the Promise of Peace, the Comforter. Mother continued to share about the bus driver who raped her. Oh, my dear mother. Bless your precious heart.

1999

April 2

Reiki session with Irene Aliotta, therapist. Inner voice said, "Put forth arms." I did, and someone took each hand. Then I heard, "You can do this because someone is behind you." I heard my own voice say, "Where is this going?" "To you" (meaning, to me). (In these experiences, I Know I'm receiving spiritually.)

2001

February 25

Dr. Richard Charron and I discussed ESP. It is the ability to read individuals – not with words, but with feelings, intuitively. It will be used in my work. I'm wondering how. Dr. Charron tells me we'll explore self–healing at our next meeting (tomorrow).

February 26

12:23 a.m.: I woke from a deep sleep to a vision. I saw a hand extended from *timeless* into *time*. I reached to the hand and received. A voice spoke, "Can I touch that aroma thing (healing) and perform that?" "Yes," I said. I saw a new vision: a speck, some color. I went to it in the light and put my finger on it. My ability to read without words, individuals I work with. They don't need to be aware of it; they heal.

A voice spoke: "Write the book."

Another voice said, "Reach for the reach. That is your only thing. Effort is necessary for writing. Do it. This book is a source of healing for the world." I was reminded of an experience that occurred during Gestalt training fifteen years earlier. I was in a bath. Words came. Visions. Experiences. A shift in awareness occurred. "Write the book. Pick up the pen. The words will be given."

I had 100 percent resistance to write, but there are no excuses. I am a poor speller and not highly educated. What would I write about?

April 15

Doug and Julie are going to have a baby. Wheeee!!!!!!

Grief: Grieving my dear Chaz.[6] How I miss you! My forever friend. The dearest in the world to me. I miss you in the morning, coming to rub against my legs. I miss your hugs to me and your embracing me from your head to the tip of your tail. I miss lying on the mat where my face touches you as I salute the sun. I miss giving you fresh water to start your day, and when you come into the kitchen for your stroking after each client leaves. I miss your adoring stare as you sit looking up at me, your guarding presence,

---

[6] Chaz was Patricia's beautiful friend.

your warm, thankful leg rubs as I prepare tuna juice or cream in your saucer, and as you patiently, silently wait for a tidbit of fish or meat to arrive in your dish after dinner. I miss you sitting on my lap on a porch or deck chair as my companion. I miss you sitting at my head on the couch between Ed and me when we watch a movie. I miss my friend, always with me as I go in and out to the porches or deck and who snuggled on my lap, your warmth soaking into me. Your wet kisses, your paw gently touching my sleeping cheek as day breaks, and the soft, softest, softer still feeling of your fur under my hand. I miss the unmistakable, pure, sweet scent I deeply inhale and your presence at the door as your sweet voice welcomes me home, dear, dear heart.

April 16: Chaz

I awoke before 5:00. The porch was newly set up for spring without my dearest companion. Rain fell. He'd be at the porch door. No Chaz. *Omubelideleu!*[7] A burst of pain. Emptiness cries out of my heart. Gasps and sobs take their turn. I knew it was time for you to leave. I saw how frail you had become. I saw the loss of your beautiful coat. I saw you lying in the middle of the kitchen floor this past month, and on the front porch, on the chaise. The bothersome car ride to the vet was unnecessary. You understand my need to be free of guilt, of not doing all that I could. I knew. I knew and did not want to accept it. You spoke profoundly to me, dear one. I knew.

---

[7] Represents what Patricia felt at the death of Chaz. Emotion and pain erupted with this sound.

A mystical moment: Then in my emptiness, you came to me. I *saw* you inside of me. I *saw* and *knew* you intimately, as I could not know you in the flesh. I recalled Jesus's words: I must go away that the comforter will come. Yes! Yes! I love you as I love my*self*. Your holy presence blessed me all your earthly life. Our Creator gave you to me as a gift. Your constant presence, attention, adoring love. Guarding me always in softness and communing love. The giving and receiving between us, the friendship, playfulness, joy – as a baby kitten who called to me from the culvert while I was on my morning jog. You were God's gift to me! You tickled my stomach… such a darling baby. You sat on my shoulder and nibbled my ear. You licked my face. God called to me from the culvert. It was His voice I heard, His touch and joy I have lived with. He has adored me and guarded me. I am precious to him as you are to me. God's voice called to me and I answered Him. I have accepted his most precious presence and joy – they are mine forever. My grief and sadness turned to joy in yet another mystical moment. Emptiness and loss became fullness and presence. A knowing of *your presence*, of your beautiful eyes on me always. I AM *always*, forever, aware of your eyes and your presence. We are One. Forever One. All who have gone before, all here now, all to come. *I AM One with all*.

April 25

I asked for the robin's message – the robin that kept flying to the window, trying to get into the house and giving constant attention to the house from the tree.

10:00 a.m. – Reiki session at my therapist Irene's house – First, I heard a loud tapping, similar to the sound of the robin at my house. The sound was continuous, though Irene could not hear it. Then, I felt a strong drawing at the top of my head. I went out of awareness. When I returned, I saw a white face. I was unable to bring back all that went on. I felt enormous, huge, globular. My hands were out of reach while Irene's hands were on my stomach. I saw a white left arm and hand. The arm was bent at the elbow, above me, and went into my abdomen. This Reiki session was long. I felt unfinished. While lying there, I saw myself on my stomach with wings on my back.

June 25

Meditation: Voice: "Be still." It was hard to stay awake. I felt a thump, as if I had put my foot down. Obey. I felt a breath starting up within me. I felt consciousness give commands.

June 26

Meditation: I saw two concentric circles next to each other. One was black and the other was white. I called them cells. This was my first awareness of seeing unrecognizable images.

July 27

Reiki with Irene: I saw two cherub faces close to mine. They were angelic, round faces, with deep eyes and curly hair. I mentally acknowledged them and wondered (asked) why they came. Then I saw my spirit self – a white image – rise up from the table with angel wings on my back in a black, velvet night, with billions of stars. I feel I am light. I felt a drawing in my physical body, in the left breast, an akashic cord connection.[8] One star focused on as coming from my back. I turned onto my stomach and *felt* angel wings move on my back. I was the angel who spoke to my mother at Heaven's gates when, at the age of thirteen, she almost died and I said, "Not yet. Not yet." I had a very natural experience and understanding of this. Why was I given this beautiful experience? Later, my son, Tom, said I may not have experienced it for a reason. Something came full circle. Whole. Yes. I feel free of responsibility for Mother. I can now love her freely.

I realized and experienced my part in the creation of myself. I could not have comprehended that any other way. I also experienced physical death when my angel spirit left my body – the actuality of so–called *death*. It is nothing more. (My heart skipped a beat.) I called Mother and shared my experience and I feel good.

A few nights ago, I told Mother I would share my past experiences with her sometime. We talked about her near–death experience at age thirteen and I asked if the angel's voice was a man's or a woman's. It was a woman's. Years ago I had a vision. I saw writing on a wall that said, "You are an angel."

August 22

Night processing: I drowned at age five. Now, years later, I am drowning again. The entire bottom of my body is chilled but there was sun on top. I thought, "I'll have to cough and clear this water out. *No.* I saw the back of myself on my right. I rose and stood tall

---

[8] Represents how we connect with other people emotionally, mentally, spiritually in embodied life.

– a very strong warrior, with a big, long, white gauze robe. I didn't see a head, but felt it to be a powerful male. I was consciously in touch with my power; now I was at one with it, I felt it. We heal ourselves of all afflictions and diseases. I *know*. I realize it.

I'm in a clay hut. The wooden door is open. I had something in my hands, so I closed the door with my foot. I said, "Ben, take care of that." Words came to me. "To close the door, you both need to be in agreement." I realized this means discrimination in healing takes place on a small level between the healer and the client. I had asked, "How would I know when *not* to heal?" The response was that I did not need to be concerned with that – the door would be closed if we were not in agreement. I saw Joseph (my first grandson) as a pixie or fairy. He was in a corner on the left, happy, smiling. He said something to someone. I turned over on the table and felt my own hand go under me. We are all one; there is no separation. I heard the words, *"I am cared for. I am cared for."*

Priests are spiritual warriors. I survived drowning, attempted abortion, and the challenges through my own power – the "*I am*."

August 30

Reiki with Irene: The top of my head was very hot. I felt the fluttering of wings again while I lay on my back.

September 12

Dream: Chaz is with other cats. I said, "He wasn't alive in the other place, but I knew he wasn't dead." His body is different.

September 14

Reiki session: I told Irene about the dream of Chaz. I know I was on another plane or dimension of Consciousness. I asked, "What good of service is this ability?" (All is given for service.) Answer: "I am a bridge." I felt very watery, emotionally fluid and not ready for this. It's too awesome. "We never are ready." So, this is my work. I don't understand it and know nothing about it consciously. "I will."

October 18

Reiki session: Irene saw a bright light come out of my head. It knocked her back with a jolt which I, too, experienced. I turned over. My head felt like it was pressing into the earth, with my feet suspended. The top of my head was hot long after Irene removed her hands.

October 29

Gestalt Pastoral Care training class with Tilda Norberg:[9] During meditation, I experienced turning counterclockwise, back to being born again, anew in every moment. Miraculous! Death was swallowed up in victory and newness. Grief turned to joy. I saw symbols: a cup in the clouds, mist, birth.

---

[9] Founder and first president of the Gestalt Pastoral Care, Inc.

October 30

Training class: Night words: As a healer, it's a case of identity.
"Who am I?" A covering was put over my head. The top of my
head pulsed. My third eye is open.

After the class session, I meditated in the chapel for three hours. I
was told inwardly to sit, not lie down. A thought came, "Edgar
Cayce gave answers to health questions while in a trance. I saw
my spine. I saw light in two areas – the fourth dorsal and down
low." I focused effortlessly and I moved my head slowly, leading
with, "There is nothing new. Cayce could. I can." I saw energy
patterns. Miraculous! And natural. An inner vision was red and
pink. I felt pain: "stretch to that pain, focus." I asked to see clearly,
have sharp vision, not binding or painful, but right vision, both
inner and outer.

November 4

Class work today included my hip. I focused my attention on my
right hip. I went into it. I felt energy in my upper body and feet,
though not in my legs. I felt like a man with no legs. I had always
been repulsed by birth defects. Tilda asked, "How does it feel?" I
don't want to go there.

Class session: Healing: Release of being a disappointment as a girl
– a failure. Mother expected a boy. He would have been called
Peter John. Our minister's wife told Mother that, if her baby was
not a boy, to name her Patricia. Divinely named. Life came to my
legs. Awareness came. When I looked in a mirror, I looked
strange, not normal. Now I see I am normal and feel I'm a strong
woman. This work was a classic example of the death layer and of

healing, though it was not as I had expected. I was in it a while and felt the turn.

I felt I never pleased my daddy. I never felt his eyes on me. (Maybe they were, but I was too ashamed of myself to look into them.) While he sat reading the paper, I sat on his lap and put bobby pins in his hair. He picked me up at the neighbor's and rode me home on his bike. I felt like a burden to him. Mother was supposed to pick me up, but sometimes she forgot. I felt a bother to her.

How did my neediness play out? Not to be seen. Never need anything of anyone. Embarrassing to need help and ashamed to ask for it. I didn't know what to ask for and I didn't know what I needed. Performance anxiety came up big. As a child, I wanted to play fighting games, not dolls. I didn't know how to play.

2007

January 27

Night notes: My left molar awakens me. What's covered up and needs light? Healing of ancestors. Family dinner was scary. Daddy came down hard on Sonny (brother Carl). Poor Sonny! I hurt for him. Daddy would grab his razor strap off the wall, march Sonny to the pantry and strap his bare bottom while we were sitting at the table eating. I feel sick to my stomach remembering it. I am just now feeling the fear and anxiety in my stomach. I was afraid to cry. I swallowed the pain and fear. I wanted to scream, "Stop it, Daddy. Stop! You're hurting Sonny. I hate you for hurting him. You're horrible!" But I was afraid to. My tongue and teeth were not in agreement. I had to bite my tongue and clench my teeth. I spoke to my tongue: "Tongue, function naturally. I will allow you to. I will not control you. I will say what I want to say now. I won't hold it in." I internalized this pain around eating. My anxious stomach did not digest properly. I asked the Holy Spirit and Jesus to our table. Light and peace came. Jesus stood between Sonny and me and said, "You are not responsible for him and cannot save him."

January 29

Healing: I asked the Holy Spirit for a new way of seeing my dad. Answer: "Give to your dad what you want." I love you, Daddy; I love you, Daddy; I love you, Daddy. I see who you are, Daddy. You never got the love you needed from your daddy. You didn't know how to give it. I run into his arms and *feel* loved. I never told him I loved him. I never ran into his arms. Fear, shame, and pain kept me from loving you, missing you, and grieving you. When you went to the hospital on Christmas Eve, I was shamed for asking if I would still get a doll and teddy bear for Christmas. It is *now* clear to me. I didn't know if you were coming back or if you were gone forever. I was confused. Christmas day was tomorrow, but would you be there? You were mean to Sonny. I was afraid of you. I never knew when the strap was coming off the wall. Then you never came back. No more strap for Sonny. No more pain for me. Just an unspeakable feeling where the pain used to be. We get used to the pain. Who am I without it at age four?

Memory of accident at age five: I knelt on a chair at the kitchen table. I invited the Holy Spirit to be with me. My shins hurt where they hurt long ago. I screamed! My arms tightened and I felt pain in my elbow and upper arms. My hips tightened as I drew back in

31

pain. Mother was grinding vegetables for relish at the table. I put my finger in to push the vegetables down the way I saw her do it. Pointer finger of my left hand got caught in the blades and ground off the nail. Now these body areas have signaled me. There is something here to look at that needs healing. Thank you, God. Oh, thank you, Holy One. Body houses my terror shock and pain.

March 1

I am at the edge of sleep. I am feeling excitement within. I am ready. Speak. "You have seen me. You know me. I am the One who came to teach you all things you need to know. Learn of me. Let nothing halt you now. You have begun. Flow like a river. I reveal myself as you can behold me. HEAR my voice in all things. It is I. Encourage everyone. Appreciate all. Humor is divine truth. It sets echoes ringing." Open space in mind. It was blank.

Realization:

GOD BREATHED INTO ME "FROM WITHIN," NOT FROM WITHOUT WHEN GOD CREATED ME.

The image of an eye: What I (eye image in). Image: I'm carrying a golf bag in hand. Keep my eye on my goal – ball in the hole – one with it. "This is a game. Have fun – enjoy it – lighten up." Thank you.

March 15

My desires and dreams: To be a clear channel for God's love to flow. This is my first. Write my experience, let it flow. I feel the soft excitement that speaks to me. I must maximize my ability to perceive Christ's vision. To be all I can be. I love to dance. I danced on a table once. I love to sing. I will sing my song. Clear, cool days make me high. To write creatively, take it lightly, enjoy it. Relax, it will come. Balance, exercise, work, rest, space, meditation. Do what I *feel* to do. Listen to self. Follow little urges, nudges, make no plans. Space allows guidance.

Extension of senses: I maximize my senses to a higher vibration, to a higher level of comprehension (understanding) and sight into the spiritual realm; inner vision. To see reality behind the appearance or symptom. I am able to look through limitations or blocks and see truth: heaven on earth; the order God created. I look with the Holy One to behold what lies behind the seeming, to judge it righteously. As I see more clearly with inner vision, my physical sight will reflect it. Thank you.

When we hear negativity spoken, practice tuning our ears to automatically reverse it to positive, in our mind, knowing the error is partial truth.

We develop a rarified sense in stillness and prayer. Rarified: finer sense of feeling in Reiki, touching a body, transferring energy which feeds the subconscious, and healing occurs. We contact the place of error in the mind. Healing and prayer is the orderly operation of vital energy, a transmitting of life when a person is actually receptive and the creation of fresh opportunity for the person by power of spiritual projection which eliminates space by ignoring it. Our lives become open for God's use. Our concern and desire for these loved ones is so great, we lay ourselves over against them that your love may move through us to touch them in healing. As we offer ourselves for its transmission, we can actually feel the current of life flowing through us. It's life that heals. Let go. Let go. Let go. In abundant life all fear is gone. Every word and feeling is sent into their subconscious reservoir to be brought up later into their conscious perception like a revelation. These words which remain in our own subconscious continue to reverberate long after we have ceased to speak them. In an atmosphere of sincerity and safety all tension is released.

March 26

Asked for more understanding of the vision of white glow behind black lines. Received a vision of a tree with a spotlight on it.

April 16

Night vision: A vessel of oil was pouring out from the left side of me. I sat up in bed, my hands cupped and raised to receive. My first passion years ago: to be a clear vessel or channel through which God's love flows. At the time, I had no idea what that would entail or mean. It is healing. Oil of anointing.

August 15

I want to be all I can be for life. When with the grandkids, I sometimes feel the tug of wishing I'd known things better with my own kids. I put this empty wish behind me. I give it to the Holy Mind, who answers me with, "You did the best you could. It was enough. You are enough, Patricia." (Even though I felt not enough for Mom and Dad when I was born.) You both loved me and I chose this. You did the best you could. I pledge my life and energy to the beneficent extension of love to my Father, Creator, God. The Holy One has given me a new perception. I am grateful.

August 20

I felt pain in my left shin and knee. I had been judged as not
enough by my daddy. I judged another as not enough. My first
perception at birth. I chose this. It was root cause. My pelvis, jaw,
hip, and knee are out of line. I understand, Daddy, and thank you
for the lesson I need to learn: Judge not. I believed I was not
enough. Women are not as good as men. *All* women are not as
good as men. Corrected. Women are as good as men. I felt
inadequate as a female, as a mother. My pain told me I am in
error, which means my feelings are not in line with the truth.

August 26

Dream: I put a large, round, hard candy in a child's mouth. I
immediately knew it was a mistake. I put my finger in but knew
she had swallowed the candy. I picked her up by her feet and hit
her on the back. I walked around in the dark, frantic, trying to yell
for help. Nothing came out. 9–1–1 will be too late. I can't take my
mistake back. This feeling matches the pain of seeing pain in my
children and feeling it is my fault and I can't take it back. I have an
erroneous feeling of responsibility – heavy, horrible, hopeless. We
are touched only by the hand of God. I remembered I did the best
I could, and it was good. I am enough.

With open eyes, images I see before me: circles within circles –
black outside, white inside. Some are black within white as well.
The circles touch, enclosed in tube-like form. The tubes are
flexible, curving, looping, extending, meeting – floating in space.
(These were the second images seen.)

Black circles, white inside, touching the inner circumference of the larger black circle. These circles are three to four times larger than the ones in tube shape and have fine lines of colored light in them.

Night notes: Vision: A hand gave me three white packages (I will know what they are when I give them, as giving is receiving). I don't open them; I open *to* them. Three in One – Trinity – three spiritual children – gifts of God.

Night notes: Vision: A shadow figure lay over me, third eye to third eye. Overcome. "I am perfect expression of God." No need to manifest error of others to correct them. Direct from heart of God. Only this.

Realization: I awoke to a pulsing in my head. An erroneous belief. I wake myself to more understanding. I am all. I know this as head knowledge and am waking to what I don't know as *truth*. I had believed that erroneous belief had power, was substance, could affect the body, and pain would be the effect, signaling to alert the mind to the error in its belief, which I then ask the Holy One my Great Self to correct the erroneous perception. Who made the error and who observed it? One is One forever. Two cannot come from One unless One is divided in two. The Spirit is One. Indivisible. Eternally.

Understanding: I had been believing in two distinct entities – the spirit and the body – calling the two by different names or forms. Where does the body begin? Where does the Spirit end? "I have wasted one hundred and thirty–four years."

I am free of a past image. Leave it and continue to move into Now. Be in now. Behold God's wonders to perform, move out of the past and allow new vision, new beauty, ever and ever–new ideal. God's thoughts are forming now as eternal awakening. Open, open, open. Allow, allow, allow – beauty, love, truth, integrity, generosity, benevolence. *Life* to bestow *itself* upon me. Things which eye hath not seen and ear hath not heard – and which have not entered the heart of man. All that God has prepared for those who love Him (My Holy Self). I expect great things to unfold – already accomplished.

Realization: I am walking with God. God is my legs. My legs are God's. I walk in God. God walks in me. The walk to God is of God and by God.

Realization: I see myself putting on a new body. I felt I was stepping into it, pulling up the legs, abdomen, chest, arms, and slipping into it. I am a new creation in Christ. I am Christ body.

Meditation: A new client comes. Can I help her? "Here are the keys to the car."[10] It was so subtle I almost missed it. So natural.

Reiki for Doug: His feet are hurting him. You are the comforter and answer, Lord. Answer: "Did you think about the light slippers?" I went right to them under the stairs. These will give him comfort and self–support.

Night notes: Thoughts: Follow the thought, stay with it. The thought takes you to the resolve or the answer. Truth. Hold to it.

Meditation manifest: I saw a left eye. A light beam projected from it. Keep my eye on the goal. The light became stone, solid, manifested.

---

[10] Car represents the client's body.

Meditation: I am living protoplasm. I am perfect balance. I am pure essence. I am living breath of God – Holy Spirit.

Morning, before opening my eyes, all is pure gold in my mind's eye.

Meditation: I heard a *D* octave – both sounds at once.

Before sleep: I had a vision – a clear, green eye – my inner vision is seeing new life. That is all there is every moment.

Night notes: Precious children, your cries of pain are received. You are growing, stretching, reaching for the prize of acknowledgement. Your colors shine through. "What about me?" "Yes, you. Yes, you." Bits of kindness and tenderness are your plea. Oh, yes, you greatly matter. I am honored to be present. Thank you for allowing me this sacred bond. As an observer, all is well. Love and goodness do I behold.

Before sleep: "How do I will thought?"[11] An image appears – two fabrics: one white, one colorful, securely joined by a seam. To the observer, they are one piece. Trust my partner. I am one with my Source. My will is God's will. Intention. Picture, imagine, feel.

Evening: I am listening to the frogs and cicadas. I hear each sound separately, not as a symphony. Intent to hear, sharply focused on steps and rhythm. Communication between selves. We are connected to all, second by second – now, now, now.

---

[11] Patricia addressed Spirit to have truth revealed.

Revelation time – I am on my porch, meditating. There is white, cloud–like movement from above. I hear a child's voice say, "My God." Bright light filled my mind's eye, with a small white circle in the center. I opened my eyes. Bright, clear bursts of light appeared in my field of vision. I closed my eyes. Everything appeared blacker than the usual grayish field I saw. I then saw a soft, glowing red, then yellow. I opened my eyes. Yellow was not a circle; it was a snowflake shape. I saw clear white bursts. A bird flew to a branch near me, then lots of birds came. Large birds – hawks, eagles – flew over trees. I felt a pulsing in root chakra and a tingling in pineal crown chakra. I closed my eyes. I saw a light turquoise circle, then red, then red–orange with yellow coming through the red. An image appeared: two thumbs holding a clear lens in a silver ring.

I saw a dot of white light then spirit faces: Mother, Uncle Bob, Abraham (from the Bible), and others. I saw a tree limb in the distance. The snowflake shape is a mandala.[12]

Meditation: Pulse in root chakra. Pulse in kidneys, up my spine, neck, and head. My crown chakra is now wide open. All chakras are open. I see a cloud–like circle of energy.

Meditation: The sound of heart in my left ear. All comes to me for learning and teaching. The physician in Self is the Great Self. I do not know how to deal with this. I allow truth to be revealed. Heart

---

[12] In Hindu and Buddhist symbolism, a mandala is a geometric shape that represents wholeness, the universe. In dreams the mandala represents a search for completeness and self–unity.

of God. I feel it and hear it beat. My heart is God's heart. Stay away from the subconscious. It's in realm of mind. Seek only that which is above: Spirit.

I AM THE HEART OF CHRIST MIND.[13] EACH OF US IS INDIVIDUAL HEART – OF ONE HEART OF GOD.

Tom says, "Wait till I get there." (His body is broken and lying on the ground. His whole body is being wrapped in foil.) Flower of Life[14] transforms Tom's body (a rectangular form covered with Flower of Life pattern). His form becomes total Flower of Life pattern.

Alyssa (my granddaughter) extends her hands. Sparks and lights shoot out to me. I hear the words, "See what you can do with this." Alyssa's energy is a challenge for her. I see myself as a six–year–old child and answer her through my child self. My eyes are deep and I smile sweetly. I can meet her on that level. I feel the warmth and peace in myself. She received.

3 a.m.: Heard my heart pounding in my left ear and I felt twinges of pain. The outside of the ear near my face was sore to the touch. It was very hot. What do I need to hear?

"My Holy One, I have called you out from among them. Listen with your heart. I AM Lord, your God Forever and ever. I want you to know me and walk in my way. I AM loving you now, now.

---

[13] Christ Mind and God Mind equate to Holy Spirit. They refer to the mind of Christ within the individual.

[14] Consists of nineteen overlapping, interconnected circles and belongs to a sacred geometry which believes all life is part of a divine plan.

My dear One whose heart I captured long ago, your willingness to be of greater and greater service echoes in the heavens. I AM training and teaching you even now as you learn to listen and hear the voice of your Lord and God, no one else, only yours. Like no other God, I AM one.

What can you do for me?

"You are doing it as you lend me your ear and I need full possession of this instrument. This means with no fear. I cannot work with fear. Be not afraid for yourself, Holy One. Your life in this body is minuscule compared to the life I have for you – the life lived in me alone, through you. You are learning my way as you express my love. A love which fills universes upon universes – so vast it leaves you dumb. I AM your life and I will fulfill your deepest longing – the desire of your heart to serve me eternally. You seem to not know what to do, your love is so great for me and our family on earth. You bring your own pain of confusion when you go ahead of me. Of yourself, you do not know what to do or how to serve unselfishly as you ask to. You cannot, but I can. Be done with questioning yourself. This diminishes my love flow through you, causing pressure and hindering your expression of Me. We are One and the same. You know this. When you doubt Self, you doubt Me.

"Learn to abide in my flawless love and being now. I AM perfect and you are perfect in me – born of my love and being. Let me take you further into my kingdom of Life Eternal. I love all my expressions through you. Your work with your brother raises you higher and higher into realms unimaginable to your human mind. My Spirit sustains and maintains you wholly, individually, and

41

completely – always – as you rest in Me. Trust Me your Self, in all ways.

"Thank you, my Beloved One. Take Me into your understanding and allow me fuller expression through my exquisite vessel. I AM pleased with you always. *EVERY STEP YOU TAKE IN MY PROMISES IS SURE AND LEAVES AN IMPRESSION IN THE SANDS OF TIME FOR OTHERS WHO SEEK MY WAY TO FOLLOW.* Rest in me. Rest. We will do still greater work as you rest in me, your Eternal Love."

Oh, my comforter, I thank you.

Night notes: God. Be a sweetness. Fulfill my taste. "I AM your honeycomb. I drip with sweetness for you."

Is that the laughing secret, Buster?[15] "Yes, it is."

November 9

Reiki: Pain. A client (Tim) feels separation from the family when he leaves to go to work. Separation from God. "How do you handle this?" Tim says, "I try to give it over to God." Try and try, but don't succeed (*A Course in Miracles?*[16]). Tim had been happy in his past life experience when leaving. Tragedy occurred and he never saw his family again. Tim said, "Why would I trust you?" "But you couldn't see the whole picture then."

---

[15] Buster was my grandchildren's dog who passed on.

[16] Spiritual thought system: The way to universal love and peace – remembering God – is by undoing guilt through forgiving.

My grandson Joe is sick. He has a cold. I called for the Holy Spirit, my Christ Mind, to share all I AM with Joe. I see a large construction vehicle pulled up in front of me. A figure was sitting on top, operating it. I was not to send Reiki (that was the first time). Knew there was a reason I was not to.

November 10

Reiki: Tim, "So what's the answer then?" You now have an awareness of not trusting God, we can ask for the answer, to have the truth revealed. This is a new realization of understanding: the answer is in the Question – Asking and receiving – Giving – are one. Transformed.

I spoke to Joe's mother and asked how he was doing. Joe gave her a thumbs up. I told his mother I had not sent Reiki, that I have been stopped from doing so. After I got off the phone, I thought and wondered about Joe and his situation. A voice told me, "It was a big job and I called in the big Guy. He came immediately and took over. Joe had pneumonia." He is healed.

November 11

Reiki session with Tim: "Why don't you answer the question? Is it because I'm so kind to you?" I feel and see energy activity. Spirit opens it. Question asked opens gift of Spirit.

We tried that in 1940. We didn't have enough electricity then to generate the spark, the light, the energy.

Female voice: I haven't been here in a long time.

Male voice: We never give up on anyone once you're in the book.

Energy, movement, spirit, answering Tim's question. What is the answer? It is never my unhealed woman. *No.* A metal pyramid appears overhead. The answer is in the question – the conflict, the feeling. Be willing to receive it – intend to receive it. Open to it – feeling. Giving to God. God cannot receive fear. Transformed in spirit. Answer is spirit. Holy Spirit is transformer. Holy Spirit within you as the transformer. Answer is in the question when it is asked. The asking opens us to transformation: movement of energy, activity of spirit. Asking generates transformer: Holy Spirit.

November 15

Meditation: I realize the spirit vision of Self. I AM an expression of exquisite feminine beauty. Hold to this that has been given. I saw a diamond in a circle of white energy and a feminine figure in a white robe like the one I wear. Isn't that silly – covering up. There is that much [of the ego]. I am talking to myself. They – the female receptacle and the male conscious mind – have nothing now (married). No, they have everything. They have each other's love. A male figure form comes through a doorway. I feel he is to be let out, to pass through, and he is. First, there is a circle of white energy with a dark center within. It is illumined Consciousness. Then there is a circle of white energy with a diamond within. The male is symbolized by the diamond; the female by the circle.

November 30

Reiki: The healing of Tom's birth experience: There was resistance. I was holding back: the doctor wasn't present. Now I'm working with baby Thomas, supporting his movement, welcoming his goal and his direction. Everything became easy. I saw Tom's light fly to the star. His destiny, his purpose – beautiful and effortless.

Night notes: "I went this way to take him"(Carl). I was pointing to the left, in a clockwise direction. "When it comes 'round, it is its own cycle of whole from the center. Everyone is." I felt understanding of this experience.

Before sleep: "*NOTHING HAPPENS INSIDE OF YOU. YOU HAPPEN INSIDE OF YOUR UNIVERSE. YOU – I – CREATE MOVEMENT.*"

Night notes: My right eye is tearing. A release of joy, of emotion. "Hide it not. You always have a right to my heritage."

My natural position as a Son of God is seeing everyone as a Son, without thinking about it, as a natural judgment. How sweet! From the Core of goodness, the heart of God. A refreshing coolness wafted over me.

IT IS NATURAL TO LEAVE THIS WORLD FULLY CONSCIOUS IN A BODY AS CHRIST DID.

Night notes, 12:30 a.m.: "You are healed because you want to heal."

Before sleep, I felt these words: "Life is lusciously rich. Living is scrumptious." They spilled out of my fullness of joy.

Night notes: I saw a figure move from dark to light. The dark was not solid, but gray with a white–like tweed. The light is cloud–white.

I *allow* the Holy Spirit to speak through me words of truth and only that. We damned the world we made through erroneous beliefs and I now set it free that I find escapes and am free to hear the Word the Holy Spirit will speak to me.

"We teach and learn one goal: unconflicted, without fear or pain." I allow His teaching to persuade the world through me, to find the easy path to God. In every circumstance I call my Self. I am a child of God. "Do you see this?"

"What?" Loud voice is mine.

"The direction you are going in your dishonesty."

"Honesty is staying close to the truth."

"I AM the ideal feminine expression of an unconditional mind."

"I'm growing inward faster than I'm growing outward."

Experience a dog, its face and nose – Flanagan.[17] "Thank you. I bless you."

Snow, a white light, our White German Shepherd who had passed on. I bless her and thank her.

"What shall I do with this experience?" "Whatever you want." I sent love and life to my family, friends, and clients – a group blessing. I opened my eyes and saw a yellow shape in a light turquoise circle.

Night notes: "There is about us a felt awareness like the green covering on the earth. The only genesis is life *itself* in expression – expressed in clear, rapid succession, instant, *now*. What do we choose *now*? The best and sweetest Life – Love!"

---

[17] Patricia's son's dog who passed on.

Night notes: "Life, Love, oozes out of us. I am a simple person. I feel extraordinary and know I am."

"I'm giving you everything backwards every morning."

"I begin again from the beginning." A clean slate.

Today is cake baking with granddaughters Sophia and Alyssa. I thrill to abandonment of creativity. They inspire my child.

Night notes: I have been working in the fifth dimension – imagination for a long time. Voices and sounds I hear I will be capable of understanding. Also working in sixth dimension – Chakra (energy centers in body). Pulsing of chakras relates to sixth dimension. Finding words to fit feeling and experience. The word *light* equals awareness in this dimension. Energy movement patterns – emptying residual love of Source from my individual mind to refill at same time – never a lack – always abundance.

I am ready to consider building a body. I feel increased awareness connection in experience and appreciation of mind as builder. Ready to explore building or undoing (correcting). I've been doing this. It's consciously clearer. Source energy is distributed through chakras. Explore Infinite energy related to other individual minds.

Sheets of energy patterns – looked like rain falling.

Night notes: "This is what I call storage. We all need a place to store things." "Keep it moving – Life – energy."

Vision: I saw a column of yellow and white cylinder–shaped light. Energy moving up. I am about direct communication with other. Pain is imagined, and awareness brings understanding.

Dream: I pick up a ticket. For where? I am given a gift. I may go anywhere.

Experience: While sending love to my brother, I saw the Hands of God. A powerful feeling enveloped me.

I am mind; I am experiencing Being mind. I AM all that *is*. Fifty percent of sleep.

The purpose of my life is to experience physical existence. My mind experiences the purpose of life in many existences. *One mind is all that is.* When I choose to be *All* that *is*, I choose.

Night notes: Dismantling and supporting, uncovering, taking apart.

Healing experience with Rachel: She lived with rods in her back and pain. I prayed to the Holy Spirit. I received these words: "She will heal. She needs to be done. I will arrange it for you." I am shy about operating on my friend. The Holy Spirit and I talk it through and I am given a vision of the work to be done. She doesn't need the rods that were put in her back years ago. They cause her pain. How can they be removed? I am shown that they are removed. I wonder in Awe and know all things are possible with God. My hand is smoothing a ruffled silver plate till it is smooth. There is a long cord extending from Rachel. I cut off the excess. I hear words. "Rods are only needed to obey or to keep straight. *It's* done. Tomorrow will be evidence." I felt a deep appreciation. "I AM diagnosing All that *Is*." Rachel came for treatment the next day. I asked, "What does this mean to you? Spare the rod and spoil the child." Rachel said, "My parents believed that was the way to treat a child. They believed harsh punishment would straighten out behavior." I said, "To you, God is a taskmaster. You do not believe you are safe from punishment."

Rachel's dream during Reiki: Three girls are taken out of a place where they feel unsafe. They will be taken to a home. Home equals God. Tell the Holy Spirit to deliver them home. Words: "It is done." The feeling of fear was removed – the rods – the punishment – the pain and fear – the feelings of being unsafe. She is Delivered.

Appreciation is the driving force for the extension of life. Vital energy is the capacity. Vitality is expression or extending. Extending and receiving are one.

Everyone comes into my life for healing. The conflict in their mind (confusion) becomes evident as a vehicle of healing the perception. Rachel heard, "You need to pay for this."

Inflamed – inspired – flame within. Spaces of stillness in writing – dance with the Holy Spirit.

Vision: I saw an eagle's head. His eyes were energy. See and feel intense piercing. There is great love for the young. Young words carried to fulfillment: expression – life – growth.

Vision: A strong, straight, tall, tall, tall tree with an opening at ground, an entrance. "I am the energy moving up this tree." I feel I am the tree and the energy. I am energy. One with All.

Voice: *"YOU ARE MADE FOR YOURSELF AS LONG AS I LIVE."* *THE CHRIST CONSCIOUSNESS.*

Night notes: An alarm softly ringing – a soft, gentle awakening.

Night notes: *"IN HEART THE HEART OF GOD IS LAID."* I heard these words within me.

Vision: I am awake with open eyes. A gigantic spider was on my right arm. I brushed it off.

Right arm (write arm) allows the creative energy to flow. I have brushed off my gift as insignificant. Spider, body figure eight – the symbol of infinity. I awaken to creative sensibilities. The world is woven around me. I am a keeper and writer of my own destiny, weaving it like a web with my thoughts, feelings, and actions.

I am a keeper of knowledge and revelations of primordial alphabet. I am inspired! Moved – touched deeply. I go to the dark places in the subconscious and my light shines brilliantly on the revisited threads of connection to cause.

Night notes: "Can I come home?"

How does one correct and transform the erroneous belief in aging body? Answer: *"I DO NOT AGE. THE BODY IS THE MANIFESTATION OF A CHRIST–REALIZED MIND, ETERNALLY CREATING NOW, NEWLY BORN FOREVER."*

Night notes, 4 a.m.: "I need you." "I am here." I went out on the deck to look up at the sky. "Speak, Lord." "I am One with all. All is One. Stop looking above. All is within." To need is to believe you don't have. We can't need something or expect what we never had. *IF WE HAD IT ONCE, WE STILL DO.*

I have no taste or preference for food or drink. I have a burning in my chest. "I want to explore this burning in my heart, dear One."

"Stop blocking me."

"Okay. I agree."

"All is well. I am nudging you. Write."

"I will. Gratefully."

Thought is capable of manifesting according to the attention we give it and the emotion we invest in it.

Illusion about the nature of Reality, that is the cause of human suffering. Contradiction of Truth. *TRUTH CANNOT BE CONTRADICTED.* That is an instance of false belief.

"You and I are One, Father

Created in the Womb of Holiness

Share One Life

Express One Love

So we are eternally."

Words given for my beloved brother Carl.

51

I experienced this revelation for Carl: Image of the Risen Lord – One with – Interchangeable. Carl and the Lord flow like waves back and forth. Felt softness, compassion, power. There was a path. It was flat; it went back to God, to home. Carl is now going back to God.

Carl asked, "Is there anything I need to do?" "Praise and honor God. Be grateful for your body and your loved ones, for nurses, doctors, medicine. Give thanks." Carl answered, "I'll do my best."

Carl had several beautiful visions and messages during Reiki. I was sitting with him before he went HOME and he asked if I saw the Angel sitting on his window sill.

Night notes:

"You do not exist. You are not apart from me."

"There is no part in existence. All is whole. Holy."

"You ordered this – eggs." (I am ready to fertilize.)

"What I order comes."

"We miss a lot of this" – what we ordered. The conscious mind is not aware of the possibility of such. Every moment we have a lot to choose from and to give attention to. Allow to grow in awareness of ever new possibilities. We need to understand the process of Life and creation.

Meditation: I see a dot of blue light, twice. The dot moves from the left to the center. Holy One, I come. I sit in you and you sit in me.

Image: A white energy heart three times. I felt and saw energy turn a quarter of the way left and down from the center of where I twice saw the dot of blue light.

There's a burning in my right breast. Eye of Horus[18] came from the left to the center (clear, spiritual seeing). This symbol has been in my left eye for several years, to my awareness, just as the Flower of Life symbol has been evident on the top of my left knee, like a seal in my skin.

Crown chakra is tingling. It is open with white light. The right side of the base of my skull is tingling, a still point.

Image of an upside down energy heart. Image of the energy heart on right side. Energy is coming from above and below and it is meeting.

I had a second of breathlessness – I felt light and lifted off. I have a burning for life and love, being with my Holy Self.

Night notes: *FROM THE FIRST SITTING OF THE ASPIRANT UNDER ILLUMINATION COMES FORTH HIS SEEING OR CONSCIOUSNESS.*

During a healing session, I fell into reasoning mind; I was drawn in. "Relate only to Spirit. Patricia's reasoning mind is useless in healing."

Night notes: *"I have been perfect all my life. I am now perfect."* Lovely vision – level land and low, tree-covered hills far out in front of me on the left. The right side is open. A peaceful scene of my life.

---

[18] Ancient Egyptian symbol representing protection, health, restoration.

Vision: A crack in the ceiling, a fine line. It is the beginning of opening to higher Consciousness.

Meditation: Forty–five minutes, though it felt like ten. I heard a strong heartbeat in my left ear. I AM in heart of God. God is in my heart. I AM eternally peaceful, aware of being alive in God and God in me. My High Self is drawing me to higher Consciousness and awareness. Crown chakra is pulsing. There is a fine, luminous movable grid, like a veil. At first, it was curtains. "I don't want those." Then I saw a fine black grid on a white background. Then, a large black hole. I went into the hole to other space – the sixth dimension. I received a new understanding of something and consciously realized the meaning of the words, the symbols from the sixth dimension. I opened my eyes and saw gold Flower of Life patterns on the ceiling.

Meditation: Crown chakra – pineal gland is active and open during all meditation and Reiki work. It is always open. I AM brought to its awareness, and have been, for many years.

Vision: Movable grid. Go to another space – the sixth dimension. Vision: A heart with white light filling it. It is my heart – God's heart. Gold energy from above.

"It's not what you think." "Oops." Tom's birth. It's what you know. Go with this. Focus on this. All else is not true. Continue moving in the path of perfection, evolving. Fear not what you think about anything. What you think doesn't matter. Stop questioning self. Listen only to Self.

Oops hid in me. I did not ask. Fear was not relieved. I must be relieved first. Holy One, I trust you to answer fear and address mistrust of doctors.

Do we want to go that path of separating?[19] Image of Andy (my son–in–law) going upstairs and watching down on me over the balcony. "The Lord bursts into own." "Wrap you up in the bud of tomorrow."

FAITH IS THE PRINCIPLE OF THIS LIFE, THIS LIFE IS LIVED BY GOD THROUGH ME. I AM GOD'S CHANNEL OF EXPRESSION. I KNOW GOD LIVES! – IN AND THROUGH ME. MY FAITH IS EVER GROWING AND EXPANDING THROUGH AND PAST BOUNDARIES WHICH DISSOLVE AT GOD'S GLANCE. GOD'S GLANCE, ONCE ACKNOWLEDGED, IS THE ESTABLISHED LINE OF LIFE, OF LIGHT IN WHICH I AM ESTABLISHED EVERMORE – MORE – MORE. I AM ESTABLISHED – SET – SECURE – ETERNALLY. I KNOW I AM LIVING LOVE. I AM JOY EXUDING AS FRAGRANCE OF FLOWER. I AM PURE ESSENCE, LIFE ITSELF. I AM GOVERNED AND DIRECTED IN ALL MY WAYS. I AM THE WAY OF GOD, PRESSING OUTWARD ALONG THE LINE (THE WAY) OF LIGHT ESTABLISHED EVERMORE. I AM THE LIVING FIRE OF ETERNAL FLAME – DIFFUSING ITSELF – BURNING EVERMORE BRIGHTLY, EXPANDING ALL I AM WHICH GOD IS. THIS FIRE – HOLY SPIRIT ACKNOWLEDGED, EXPERIENCED – ALIVE – BURNING IN AND THROUGH ME. LIFE!

---

[19] From truth; away from truth.

Night notes: "She's standing in a field of receptivity, holding a flower."

"There was such a field as that."

"We are finding it's a field of lower pressure."

"Back to Kathryn Grayson." (lovely voice.)

"Would out."

"Steve [Tom's childhood friend] is on his way home."

Ed is sitting in a throne chair. "When are you coming home after this?"

Before sleep, "Give me your thoughts." Image of Donna – a red rash over her right eye. She's a seer. "I AM turning you upside down, shaking you out."

Night notes: "I AM in direct line with my highest good," (looking up through bodies of substance). I feel and experience being in direct line with my highest good. I AM going into action – Saturday coupons.

Realization: I have called you and you have come to me – I trust you – My faith is in your faithfulness to me – I know you intimately – You have made yourself known unto me – You have come to me – I consciously received you – You are with me evermore. (This was an exchange with my Self.) I felt the softening

56

when the Spirit spoke. My words were empty and cold until they were spoken by the Spirit. They melted me.

I adhere to your promise. You never leave me. A sure – you are sure. You give me to understand. There is no sacrifice, no suffering (fear, doubt). Understanding – solid ground. Now I feel you, trusting your Promise. This I understand: You are the Promise.

I hear my mother's words: "We're managing." Strike that! "You have credit. I will do that for you on your account."

"You are my account – ability – endless, eternal power, life abundance pouring forth, overflowing my cup with goodness. All good. Pour forth liberally great abundance.

Wealth – affluence – abundance – Profusion – Power – working power – mind – More – more – more – ever More of Life."

My love. This is destroying you. Hold to gentleness. Breathe in the freshness. Taste Its ever newness of Life. Behold your Self. Once strapped in, they are ready for the ride. This is most gracious. I give you all my Self.

My most precious One. This is what we can do for each other. This is how we build each other up. You are sealed as my own, my everlasting One. It doesn't matter if he falls apart. I keep all the pieces together. Life renews itself continually. Life follows life.

A song is given, represented by the following musical notes:

I shall come to you in happiness.

D G B A B A G E D

I shall come to you.

D G   B G A

I shall come to you in happiness.

D G B A B C B A G

I shall come to you.

G A B A G

I have important news to tell you. There is a large eye, then energy movement from the left. You are not apart from me. You do not exist. There is no part in existence. It is a dark color – yes, indeed. It can be erased. You will be ready to pass forevermore. And, frankly, there's nothing left of anything. These great big elephants are trying to walk out at the same time. Oh, Holy One, realize the truth about all things. You (false self) don't know your Self.

Tickling in root chakra. Help in understanding. This is great. Thank you. Your eyes are opening. They are open. They are open. They are open. Patricia says, "I don't know that much." Well, sure we do. [We are] six million years old. This is life here. The vagina and the mouth – they are receptacles – eyes – they take in. "Something is waking up within me." Spirit's voice: We just turned on the sixth light. "What are you talking about?" I feel an inner burp and pressure in my inner left ear, a sharp pain. Spirit: That's life until we open it up again.

Do you remember what I did? I set the stars in the sky for you. Everything, I have given for you. Why? Because of Love, that you may know of Love – my Love. Do you know what the stars are? They are living lights, that you may find your way through them, back home again. They are a path. All things are for you, my beloved One. Enjoy the splendid playground of your mind. Enjoy! Live! What would you want for your child?

Set pain aside. Just set it aside; it is nothing. The stars are yours. Do it. Where is aside? Where? You can't find it. It is not.[20] But you must do it – literally do it. Act in your mind. Really do it. Where is it when you reach for it [the pain]? Be aware! All of your awareness – all – bring it to the pain. The pain is gone – nowhere to be found.

See yourself as a Giant, playing in the sky. You are. Whatever you see, you create. Accept this. Clothe yourself with light, for this is what you are. Do it. Do this and live. This is your heritage. Feel it. Your light struck from anything. You are light. Think on this.

Turn around, inside out, outside in, upside down. Think. Play! Let no one cover you or stop you – no one can. Only you stop yourself.

Explore. It takes such little awareness to do this. To right all life. Be the hand of God. Feel this in you, my dear one. It is your heritage as my child. My love for you. You are a raindrop, a sunbeam, a rainbow – all. It is before your eyes now as you see it. Now.

Where is tired or pooped now? It isn't. This is [grandson] Fletcher. This is a child. This is you. Like you are picking berries from Heaven – light,

---

[20] Pain is not, because pain does not exist.

59

gentle. Allow your thoughts to go there. It knows where it is. It goes directly to it. Touch – touch – touch. Connect – connect – connect. Whole – whole. One – one. I KNOW YOU.

Dream: Doug is dead, Tom announced. Ed is walking toward me. We are in an empty space. Ed's eyes met mine – he is very grave. I could not cry out loud but was sobbing within. I longed to go to Doug, to be with him. Great. You can come anytime. It's open. A priest in a white robe with a purple train. Doug's countenance, happy, smiling, full of life. His past has been embedded.[21] It is not what it seems to be. I am correcting something – an error. Watch and see. Stay close. Let it happen. All is Self–correcting. Sooner or later a light will shine in our face. Balance in movement may have caused this within the whole.

Stuck in the day of departure [from the womb of life]. Once realized, we move. We will no longer ever be stuck.

See yourself from your center. Observe your myriad of selves at work or evolving.[22] World wholeness. Balance. Homeostasis.

Good is Now. In the process. There is no better.[23] What is now, *is God, Good,* expressing.[24] Allow. Observe from center.

---

[21] Enclosed closely in, or as if in a matrix; to make something an integral part; lacking nothing essential to completeness; light; to prepare a microscopy specimen for sectioning by infiltrating with, and enclosing in, surrounding matter (Webster's Dictionary).

[22] Eastern philosophies say we are continually changing and adding balance and evolvement to mankind.

I am doing something impossible. I asked why. Because I will do the impossible.

Awoke 3 a.m. to a thought of fear. *"THERE IS NOTHING TO FEAR."* I felt and heard the words and received immediate peace.

"MY HOLY ONE, I AM WITH YOU ALWAYS IN ALL THE WORLDS THAT EVER WERE OR EVER WILL BE."

Meditation: This (white energy circles) is the color of the Christ Mind expanding from within. I allow unfoldment of true sight. I AM awareness of true sight, insight. I honor and delight the *SELF I AM.*

Granddaughter Holland saw Jesus yesterday at Mass.
He came out of a rose.
It is the most wonderful thing that has ever happened
to Doug or his family.

Night notes: Light is issuing from an eye in a steady, continuous stream. God is the light in which I see.

"YOU DO NOT EXIST. YOU ARE NOT APART FROM ME. THERE IS NO PART IN EXISTENCE." I saw myself fly over something – a

---

[23] Life can get no better than it is right now; our continual changing creates balance in life.

[24] As God is Spirit, it must manifest itself through individuals.

rock? I said, "Did I just fly over that?" It was so easy, so effortless and natural.

To the degree we leave the relative, we enter the absolute. To the degree we enter the absolute, we leave the relative.

My contingency is right here – quota, part, share.

Image: a screen of light filled with black dots, openings; veil is not solid. I live in all mind – Spirit is All.

I am teaching this. We forget who we are. Image of me sitting at a desk. We are remembering who we are. We lost touch with who we are. We are getting back in touch with our Selves.

Experience: A male figure walking a few steps in front of me in the dark. I walked up close next to him and put my arm around his back. He put his arm around me with his right hand on my hip, drawing me closer. Act as though I am, and I will be.

Night notes: Image: a metal water pipe with vapor coming out of it, but the vapor is not moving. "I will go with you as far as you go." Must deny past wish. Thought, I can't do it – "Denial must be spiritual."

I am in tune with Love – there is no strain to a tune.[25] "Free of jail."

"Kids born today are fully integrated." We must not be angry at them when there is nothing to be angry about.

---

[25] When we are love, love is all. There is nothing else.

"I am an open vessel [I saw a boat filled with fish] receiving and offering truth."

"Remove the cloak."[26] Whatever I put on, it covers up, is false.

Night notes: A large book is placed on a desk where I am sitting. Understanding of all things is brought to me. I heard softly and weakly, "I'm not really clear." "Who said that?" I AM clear. I must be clear. I AM all there is. I argue for my Self, not against my Self.

There is nothing to argue against – I'm not split. *I AM ONE, I AM CLEAR* about my Self. "I have understanding of all things." I AM understanding of all. I AM all.

"I'm not pedaling down that road again. That's not where I want to go." It is hard work to do it yourself.

Night notes: "Weakness is not knowing for sure, good." "I keep my mind from slipping."

INTUITION AND UNDERSTANDING TOGETHER IS HEALING.

"This is the wheel of fortune. We all won. Are you in town?"

Night notes: Vision: A king's chair and I was standing to the right side, behind it. I was unable to see the complete side.

I asked the Lord for help before falling asleep. I wake to words that are sounding from within me. Not my voice: "Stand forth." I felt an internal struggle. "Let it out. Let go of it. Let it lift above." I rise three dimensionally.

---

[26] The cloak hides truth.

Image of a dragonfly with five wings on each side equals ten equals one. Its right side is alight with rainbow colors. They sparkle. Its left side is gray. Focus on the right side and allow it to bring life to the left. See it as One body, not divided, All connected to Life. I felt and experienced this, realized Truth, stillness, no movement, peace.

"You hate people." Fear is hate, not love. Now he is not himself. He is all alone. Up to now is total love. Now get this: *Total love is all.*

That idea is nice. Why does he like it? It perpetuates life. Keeps it going. I have been One Son my Whole Life. It holds the world together.

It would shatter apart if He took His mind from it. You already have this answer.

Meditation: On the beach at Lake Sacandaga Reservoir. There is pink in a blue sky. The air is filled with lights. Light energy is rising. Clear. Screen – the face of Christ. Light energy is forming, collecting. The earth is clear. Gold flower. The flower is unfolding. Alyssa moved from right to left. "Stay and play, Nanny." I open my eyes and see a gold flower.

While reading I felt called to meditate. The top of my head was tingling and I saw energy flowing from my face. It was the first time I experienced this. I went to the lounge chair and images came immediately. "Yes, I ask for more understanding and am ready to receive." I was aware of, felt and saw, energy lifting up in me. I saw a large eye in a clear space with black circumference. That outline disappeared as I claimed it within me and followed inward. There was no limit. A fabric covered entirely with tiny spirals. They became small hearts, then Eye of Horus, then yellow energy masses moving on white. I understand this gift, like all gifts, is not for use. The gift of Holy Spirit uses me. In accepting the gift, I am the gift. I'm aware of energy settling down on me from above. I saw a grid. It had a tile–like look, only more distinct. White blocks stood out from black outline in three dimensions. An eye enlarged to no circumference. Flower of Life pattern covered an endless scene. A rose became a bouquet of various flowers in a cluster. I saw coarse, pink fabric of a loose weave. Voice: "She didn't understand." I'm aware of energy lifting up. Tiny, clear, sparkling lights appeared everywhere. Tiny lavender–blue lights. A green spray of energy, white energy above and on top of my head. A pupil of eye inside me. A circle with energy streaming out. *I am gift of seeing.*

I awoke to an intense burning in my left elbow. Thank you for waking me. I heard, "I am dying. I'm not going to make it." "What? Where did that come from?" (I realized the words came from my unborn child who was nearly aborted. I lived that fear and doubt over and over again throughout this lifetime – asking to be heard and healed. I see clearly. I understand. Thank you, dear Self, for coming forth.)

Bells ringing. Wake up – felt a tingling through my body. I consciously embody life. You speak clearly, Lord. I hear and understand – all there is – Life – every cell. Flesh is a covering – Life expression, alive, Being in and through me. In Life I live and move – *I AM* – I express.

Night notes: "There is no more hill."

Night notes: "When you learn this game, you are building your skills."

Night notes: "You probably aren't much man to understand. Ha, ha, ha."

"Beyond the stars." Image of turkey chicks walking in a line in front of my house. A great harvest from Mother Earth, the womb of God – my womb.

NEVER LOOK AT WHAT I DO NOT WISH TO EXPERIENCE. CHOOSE TO SEE WHAT YOU WISH.

Night notes: "I changed. I will not change again." I changed my mind once from belief in error to belief in One power.

"How are you? Good?" Right, right, the same. I AM right–minded.

Night notes: "No one will be relieved before I by God."

"I have come to bring Life. I have come to Love."

"Change the mind of its picture. Replace it. I AM come to plant the seed of Life, to bring to mind the Living mind.

It is just a little thing, this seed of Life. Keep planting it over and over again.

I AM Perfect Life. I AM perfect place. I AM perfect faith planted in you now.

I AM Perfect Word. I AM Perfect Thought, issued forth from the center of your Being.

I AM clean. I AM clear. I AM pure. I AM Harmony spoken to you in song and color. Fling wide, oh windows of my Soul! Fresh, clean air flows through you. Taste me."

"I erase what I don't want in the picture until it is the outline of my thought.

I awoke to: "*YOU ARE HEALED.*" "You are not. You are not." "Pay this bill." "That is ridiculous. It is springtime and I don't need this blanket. It is not necessary now."

"Thank you, God. You are my life. I receive this life joyfully." Spirit body senses an idea which flows and circulates life through it and then it is complete. Healing is revealing an idea already perfect. Because we consciously acknowledge it and it is.

Morning on the deck: There is gold light around my left hand. Subconscious.

Night notes: "I have to learn." What I experience is for learning – what comes into expression through me is how I learn my mind and understand.

"*I AM HELD IN THE ARMS OF GOD*" – FLESH, BONES, PHYSICAL A HUMAN BEING. "Yes, I AM speaking. You don't speak."

I feel what I hear as movement – vibrations in Spirit. My spirit receives from Great Spirit – the Word spoken in me.

I don't take in a word. Word comes from within and expresses out. Thank you is spoken within. Felt appreciation. *Holy* is heard – experienced. I honor and respect my Self.

I feel pain in my left knee and on the outside of my left hip. Keep the leg straight and it won't hurt. I tell my Gestalt clients: Expecting to heal is striving. Be in *now* where healing happens. Be present. Yes. I am. Healing is not in the future; it is now, it is done already.

Night: Leg pain is severe. One spot is intense. My body feels anxious and wants to jump out of its skin. I asked Holy Spirit's help, perception.

I awoke at 3 a.m.: "I am here for you." I had a flashback to a bike fall at age seven. As I was turning around in soft sand, I lost control of the handle bars. The metal bar came back and hit my left knee. (There were no hand grips on the bars.) My knee was bleeding. I was in horrible pain and afraid. Mother bandaged my knee and told me to keep my leg straight so it doesn't break open. [It was a strain and fear to do that at night].

I felt pain in my elbow from a finger injury. I also had pain in the back of my right shoulder. Pain can be covert, acute, overt. Covert pain is hidden in the unconscious, masked, resisted. It can be spiritual, physical, mental, emotional. The pain in my left sacroiliac joint was masked pain for Donna. I can now deal with resisted pain. I ask to embrace it. When we resist pain, we curse it; we do not bless it.

I bless the individuals in my family, naming each, by the power of All that *IS*. I bless the water they drink, the food they eat, the air they breathe. While blessing my family, I realized I *felt truth*. I was already blessed. I acknowledge what *is*. By extending blessings to my family, I am blessed.

While preparing fruit, I *heard* the bowl crack, but I could not *see* a crack. Two weeks earlier, while walking barefoot in the yard, I heard and felt bones in my left foot crack. My foot healed instantly. I was in total awareness of it and my mind flew right to it. A physical experience will concentrate creative energy on what is physical (Dr. Charron confirmed this).

Ed and I were reading *A Course in Miracles*. Something spoke to me and I was digesting it aloud with Ed, but he wanted to get on and finish the chapter. I asked the Holy Spirit for a new perception, and then broke out in hilarious laughter. I saw myself in a new way. I experienced the perception, a step beyond understanding intellectually. I *felt* it. I had attacked Ed by choosing to feel hurt or pain ("poor me"). I saw Ed as separate, not interested. He closed the door. I felt abandoned, *dropped!* This feeling matched what I used to feel when Mother dropped me off at a neighbor's on her way to work; sad, separated, she closed the door and just left. It was a healing of the experience of Mother leaving me.

I addressed the Holy Spirit: Judgment is the big lesson I am here to learn. My father judged me as being not enough. Why? My name was to be Peter John after my dad's father. I got it! He was disappointed he couldn't honor his father by naming a son after him. Had he judged his father? Yes. My dad had to leave home young to come to the United States. He missed his family. His father missed him but knew the son he loved would have a better life. He said, "Go." This is how I felt with Doug. I realized I was speaking as my dad's father. I am allowing him to heal, to forgive and to bless my father's line. I had been intentionally blessing the lineage, but had no conscious understanding of how I was involved. I love my son and he knows it. The light has come. The line of pain: roots with twisted ends.

One son was depressed, feeling helpless, stupid. *Stupid* was his dad's favorite word. I never heard it used in reference to this son, only the other. I was never available for him in his pain and saw only the positive in him. I was blind to the negative. He's right. What can I do for him? His pain and anger are justified. What am I not seeing? What is fear blocking? I want to own my part in this. I feel awful when my son feels bad. I need to heal. I need new perception, to see things differently. How was my protecting of the positive a negative for him? I wasn't available in my heart; my head was in denial. I never saw his pain. I never acknowledged he had a problem or pain as a child. As it is justified, our pain must be acknowledged. I was afraid to connect to my son's pain, afraid to acknowledge the negative. I believed I had to focus on the good, on God. And now again, I'm afraid to feel his pain. I feel sad when he's in pain. I want to be happy but, what am I to do? I don't know what to do. I'm in a place with him of not knowing. Through love, I entered his place of pain and confusion. As a child, he felt responsible for my happiness. He could never have a problem or feel any pain. He felt my unhappiness. I would feel less than capable and did not know what to do. He had to be perfect. That's how I perceived him. Yuck! Oh, God, how awesome are your ways! How definite is your work. Humbly, I bow before you. Thank you, beautiful son, for your presence in my life. I had felt responsible for your problems. They were my fault and I couldn't face that. But, that was not true. It was no one's fault, but just an understanding of the process of life and the desire to be right versus wrong. Just be. Just be. It is not ours to judge. Just be open to feeling – enlivened, awake – twisted roots impede.

Sitting in quiet. Deep, emotional awakening. I reach one hand to the Holy One, the other to my son. He grabs it. He's got a *hold* of it, a *sure hold*. I felt it. Thank you.

Dream: I'm on a path. There is a flat stone ledge on my left side. A woman stops me and asks a question. I answer her and am feeling things of hers: a book, on the ledge. I comment on soft, moist, warm, green growth I feel with my hands. She asks where, and when I look, I cannot find it (cannot substantiate or prove spiritual consciousness). It's dark. I want to turn and continue on the path. The woman is in my face, breathing. I hear her and feel her breath on my face. She is checking me out subconsciously to see if I am telling the truth, as a lie detector, a truth sensor. It's a clearing so I can turn and go on.

I am this sensitive woman. I stop Patricia on her path because she has consciously asked if she's following her heart path and I am her subconscious, revealing her answer. Patricia feels the book I am writing; and feels the soft, moist, warm, green growth she is encountering. When I ask her where, she can't see it with her physical eyes because it is dark. She needs my light to prove it true. When she wants to turn and continue on her path, I am in her face, a breath, the Holy Spirit. She feels and hears me on her face. She knows I detect only truth, like a truth sensor, like a dog sniffing out the truth. I cleared her, assured her, that she is on the right path. We will go on together. She is sure. She knows. I AM guarding and guiding her.

Dearest Heart, I have a slight question – tiny, but big. Can I do this? I have no idea of what my life will be like. How can I function in this world? How can I relate to my family, my friends? It must be possible. It must be the only way to really live life. You know all my needs. This neck pain, this nagging ache, is for you and for fullness of Joy and Life, for constant truth. Why is it scary to fall into the hands of my God, my Creator? You have given me glimpses; you have prepared me. You have guided me; you have called me home. How can I not respond and follow? Yet, I hold back. Help me, Holy One. I give my decision to you. Decide for me.

I hear: My desire has been to be a clear channel through which your love can flow unobstructed. Answer given: I am good enough to receive God's love unhindered.

Forgiveness of illusions. True empathy. I am not alone and I would not intrude the past upon my guest. I have invited Him and He is here. I need do nothing except not interfere with my old past perception. Humility is strength in that I recognize that I do not know and accept the fact that He does know.

Offer empathy to Him. I would share His perception and His strength. I am One with All. This is Strength. The power of love lies in its Strength, Oneness, Holy, Wholeness of God that hovers over it, silently blessing it by enveloping it in healing wings – wings softer and more fragrant than the velvety petunia or rose.

Open myself to His perception by asking. This, I desire to share.

2012

I am kayaking with Ed on Sacandaga Reservoir. An enormous butterfly six inches in diameter flew to me, then directly up and disappeared. At sunset, I saw an image of the butterfly – its actual size – with a black and white lace veil covering it.

Night vision: I go to the ledge above the door and my right hand picks up keys. This action is repeated. These are the keys to life, to unlock the door. I have them in my hand. I reached for them. I will use the keys and unlock the door.

Night notes: "You are pure intelligence." I want what I know I have. I choose to express my Self – what I know. When I choose to believe it, it is so. I choose to believe I am perfect. I am perfect.

"THE DIVINE PROPERTIES OF LIFE ITSELF ARE BEING SEEN IN THIS EXPERIENCE OF MOVEMENT."

Roll with me slowly. "Stay with me." I can't leave you. "Let thought lead. Follow it."

Properties are traits or qualities belonging to, or especially peculiar to, an individual or thing – an effect that an object has on another object or the senses.

Virtue: As per Webster's Dictionary: An attribute common to all members of a class (such as race); something owned or possessed;

the exclusive right to possess, enjoy, and dispose of a thing; something to which a person has a legal title; an article or object used in a play.

"Fine. Then you're ready for the outstanding." Merit – capacity to act. Virtue – beneficial quality or power of a thing – strength. These are God qualities.

"To keep myself clean."

I am having less difficulty turning over in bed. I feel hip pain across my low spine – more severe, especially when sitting.

My right hip feels it might give out when I'm walking. I talked with my daughter. I can't trust my hip; I can't depend on it. A more conscious understanding is being revealed through this condition.

Race mind belief is erroneous. Women give birth to humans. We are spiritual beings. God births spirit through us and clothes us with the mantle of flesh. We do not make our bodies or any other bodies. We *are* God stuff, mind, imbued with Spirit, God principle – law does all through us. Everything is His expression. No wrong or error has ever been done or ever could be done. All is God. This is God's world.

I felt a sharp pain in my right shoulder (writing arm). Ed gave me Reiki. I asked for help. "Realize what you are doing to yourself." I am open to realizing truth. I believed pride went before a fall. That was an error. "There is no such thing as pride. There is only good." I've been looking for what makes sense. "That is the wrong place to look. God – all good is beyond sense. It is Grace – pure grace." I live and move by God's grace and being. Trying to figure it out is error. It is senseless. Trying to puff up ego. *Stop.*

"I AM NOT A BODY DOING ANYTHING." "WHO AM I?" "WHO ARE YOU? I AM. I AM THE REST OF YOU. THIS THING ETERNAL. I AM PROTECTING YOU, PERFECTING YOU INTO FOREVER, GOVERNING YOU, GUIDING YOU."

This is the day the Lord has made.

Discomfort in my left hip. Meditated. Help, Mighty One. "How about Self?" "Do you drink by yourself?" What do you mean? Of course. I was handed a glass and told what it was. It contained something natural. I saw electricity shooting from my head. "Honor, honor, drink of honor."

I am the queen of heaven – simply because I have overcome temptation. I was tempted to sink into human discomfort and judgment. I did not yield to it.

Night image: Profile view of me looking into a clear bowl held vertically in my right hand. The bowl is empty. "Doctor [Joseph] Gascho, I've been trying to get in touch with you. I want you to know I am here." "Know I *am.* Accept me. We are always in touch. You cannot leave me nor I leave you. We are one fabric, one substance, one Consciousness – one life eternally."

Four a.m.: I woke to the sound of the phone ringing in my mind. I am awake. I'm listening. "I am unfolding within. I share all I AM with All in my awareness." A hand reached in from the right and my awareness went to it instantly. It was Kay's call for help.

75

Five a.m.: Before waking, I experienced being moved ahead in energy (spirit) on my left. I saw energy in the shape of a block moving out and forward like a space on a playing board. Kay was in the hospital. She was seriously ill. I had not been told.

Yesterday, I felt a burning in my left leg, which I accept for good. I am open to more awareness.

Night notes: "The God Mind created the body. Our own open awareness narrows into this shock to higher awareness. Shh. Be quiet, leg, and listen to me. I am here. Enter into my silence, into me. I *am*."

Nonjudgment – Intuition to see every individual expression of life as Essence (Christ) in place of what my eyes or memory tell me; to *feel* truth behind the image.

To correct error or pain, ask, "Is there anything to correct?" It is self–correcting as I bring my attention to it. *Feel* it. *Focus Awareness.*

Blocks – misdirected energy becomes beneficial.

"Two old friends meet." "Love is using someone." God – Love using one. Our attitude is our willingness.

 I can now deal with resisted pain. When we resist, we curse; we do not bless. Embrace and transform.

Night notes: "Keep the secret. God is within us. We are in God– One. We keep faithful to the law of attraction. Ray gave her a tiny baby sister. Ray did not leave her alone. You have known this forever. Let it be. Intuitive – new knowledge. Know – One with all creation. Ray – light of Mind – Born in me. I AM begotten of the

Father. I want you to feel I AM here for you in your pain, feel one with all creation. Tell others. Baby – new birth in awareness of feeling One with all, greater awareness of the gift of intuition. Use it consciously. I can't stay any longer."

Reiki session for sister Evelyn lasted three hours. I saw an eye, then another eye opening to part of Consciousness. Two planes (of consciousness) merge. Evelyn saw a tree and large magnets. Her feet were burning and she wanted to get away. As I moved (my hands) up her body, there was not a place that did not need healing. I asked, "What happened here?" Evelyn knew (remembered) how she was injured. I saw a bone split in two; the edges were raw and out of line. Red was merging in from the edges. I felt – saw – heard shifts within Evelyn's body. There was lots of crunching and movement as it all lined up. Evelyn had a torn rotator cuff in her right shoulder. She, too, heard and felt the shifting of bones, though it was without pain. I saw an image of a glowing Star of David and then prehistoric animals: elephant, triceratops, and others – walking fish in water, small gray and white animals running. The view was miniature. Far in the past, but clear. When Evelyn's session finished, she was able to raise her right arm, an arm that hadn't moved in twelve years. With practice, she could have full use of it in time, lifting it higher and higher. It all seemed natural. Evelyn was not excited so much as she was amazed.

Long distance [phone] Reiki with Evelyn[27] to address her dry mouth. During her session, she swallowed three times. I felt a drawing from the root chakra to the center of my abdomen. I saw

---

[27] Time, distance, space do not impede the Reiki healing process.

a woman washing vegetables in a strainer and a man with salt and pepper. I saw hair part and a small, white fetus appear. I felt a tingling in my upper right lip and also nose – smelling, sensing, and tasting memories of past. Evelyn had tears in her eyes. She had not cried, nor had she been able to cry, in years. This was more healing.

Night notes: I see a white semicircle on the horizon. It is my subconscious light rising. I saw granddaughter Sophia's eyes. They were deeply focused. She asked for the tape.

Night image: I saw myself stepping out of my body, as it was falling down. Let go of the image of Jesus as a man. Christ Mind is not meek, but power. With my eyes closed, I see light. When I open them, I see rectangular gold light. It looks solid rather than like moving energy. Thank you for this gift and for making it known to me. I am seeing Source energy and opening more and more to it. Thank you, God–Source.

Night notes: Experience: I woke and saw a Lion walking, full life size, close enough to touch. I felt and sensed myself as Lion – natural, whole, capable, peaceful, gentle, quiet. Paws touch the ground – power – gentle. I was looking out from within the Lion. I felt one with all – the earth, sky, air, and water. I am Lion. Lion is in me.

Dream: I am in a mansion with many women servants. The owner of the mansion gave me the keys to a car – a roadster with no top (convertible). The owner told me to take his car to get where I am going. When I sat in the car, servants came to me. One said, "You can go anyplace with that." She pointed to my necklace. I looked at it. It was a large gold symbol hanging from a chain. I looked at the woman and knew she spoke the truth. She brought it to my conscious awareness.

Night experience: In bed. I opened my eyes. There was light all around me. I turned to see if Ed had turned a light on. He had not. I heard a bong–bong–bong sound that went on and on. With the first bong sound, the light was gone. My clock said 9:33. The bongs continued. I went downstairs to look at the mantle clock. I played F on the piano. I heard a far and close sound – an octave – then both sounded at the same time. I sat on the porch, closed my eyes. Two large eyes peered at me. The one at my right side opened and I felt myself enter it. I felt a strong pulsing through my body. My next awareness was to feel a drawing sensation (like the force of a magnet) tightening from the center of my throat up the side to my jaw. End of experience. At 11:45, I returned to bed. The chimes continued. When I awoke the next morning, the chimes had stopped. Time is no more.

Night note: I woke and saw a finger pointing up above me. "I need to tense."

Night experience: Sophia opened a door to me. She was smiling and inviting.

Night note: My ear woke me. I am open to nonpersonal Deity.

I accept Source as my Deity, my God. I feel acceptance of Source as my Deity. I feel total acceptance of feeling One with Source.

Love of Source. I am creating new patterns of creation. Deconstruct unconscious. Construct consciously.

I am looking at clouds out the window. I stopped them by focusing again and again.

My image patterns are a piece of holographic film containing encoded message.

Regeneration of bone is rare because achieving it requires accessing very deep levels of psyche that are not reached through normal levels of consciousness. Emotions felt during events are recorded in the cosmic hologram. The emotional intensity of an event makes it more prominent in the hologynic record, allowing the individual to tap into them.

Feeling one with All means gaining All that IS – losing nothing and retaining individuality. I am a fish in the river of the composite all.

I speak life-giving words. My thoughts are creative. They come through clear, not worked over. They are New – fresh – constant movement in *NOW* – present.

Night notes: My voice, "You want healing on the mind level. I heard you." There are rainbow clouds, attention to the second toe of my left foot. Eye to eye – touching eye. My eye reaching out to touch other eye. Vision.

Night: Teleporting: Images and experiences are more intense. Before sleep, a thought came. I will be operating on the brain. I am open to this; no learning has blocked it. I am seeing and sensing in another dimension. Lots of faces and a strong, clear light. One side is like a beam of fog, the other side is clear. I am Ready. I am back and aware of breath. Each time, I felt my chest several times, for a short time. Did breathing stop? When I'm gone, the body needs less. Felt and saw the face of God in the clouds? Tongue was out – people were walking into mouth. Then lips pressed closed. I saw a forehead of a face – cobalt blue – light intense over scene: birth of Christ in a manger. Multicolored lights to the side.

My work is teaching – receiving, giving, sharing what I learn with clients.

Night vision: I am being served three prepared foods on a tray. "The Lord is all goodness."

Awakened by my voice. *"I AM LIFE WITHIN YOU. YOU ARE MY EXPRESSION. I FILL YOU COMPLETELY. YOU CANNOT HOLD ME IN. OPEN WIDE THE HEART OF LOVE, OF LIFE. I RACE THROUGH YOU. YOU BEHOLD ME, WITNESS ME IN YOU. I MOVE IN AND THROUGH EVERY THOUGHT YOU THINK. I AM THE BEAUTY YOU SEE AND FEEL. I ECHO AND RE–ECHO THE WORD OF TRUTH. I DO THIS. I TAKE HOLD OF YOU AND SCATTER YOUR SEEDS OF LIFE WHERE I WILL THEY GO. EARTH IS MINE, AND THE FULLNESS OF."*

2013

January 1

I AM a miracle. I am. I. I. I. I. I. Today is a brand new day. Each day is the start of the first day of Eternity. This very day. It is a holy day, a holy instant. Grace. Grace. All is Grace.

January 6

I AM the Light in which I see. I see in God's light. I see in love. An answer true.

January 7

I felt pain in my right shoulder on and off today.

Mediation in the afternoon: I am lying down. My shoulder hurt so badly, I wanted to get away from it. I addressed Holy Spirit's help. I am open to truth regarding this shoulder. What is it telling me? Where is this error in my mind? I can't do anything about the pain. Help. I want truth. Correction.

Answer: I pinched a nerve when I fell yesterday. I went outside to throw away greasy water from a pan. While doing the dishes, I reflected on dinner. I wanted to please the children, but I found making decisions to be challenging and painful. I was afraid of making a mistake, that it wouldn't be what they wanted. My daughter–in–law, Deb, said I couldn't do that, but I try regardless. Daddy died. I didn't want candy. I wanted Daddy. It's Christmas again. This time, Carl's gone. I felt a loss of power, that I had no power over death. Thank you. I was convinced of this at the age of five. I believed it unquestioningly all these years. Death was the victor of life. I worked this out through my attempts at making the "right choice." Not having what I wanted (i.e., Daddy) drove me to give others what they wanted. For the time, I lived in their happiness, every time, again and again. My wrong choice was an acceptance of death as the end of life and happiness. I was guilty of choosing my doll and teddy to bring me happiness. I will ask Tom for help.

I had fear of germs, infection, bone loss. Holy Spirit, I'm open to the truth. I want to trust you completely with *all* my life. Answer: How can there be not enough of anything? Can there be lack in the mind of God? There is more than enough. Rest assured. Is there infection? Impurity? Impossible. God is pure, clean, clear, innocent, childlike. Thank you, Holy One.

After studying and practicing *Creative Mind*[28], a thought came: *I ABSOLUTELY ACCEPT THESE EYES (I'S) ARE NOW SEEING CLEARLY, DIRECTLY FROM THE HEART OF GOD.* There is nothing to obstruct perfect vision. There is only God.

January 18

I gave up wearing glasses. Reading is slow. I now read to focus on each word. I told Ed I appreciated his patience with my reading. He asked, "How's it working for you?" I realized it was working exactly as is right. Because I need to focus, I allow the word to unfold in me. I take it in. It is the inner vision. I enfold the word. I brought up the issue to address. Yes, Ed's question was correct and in line with the issue.

January 21

Sat with Tom. Low back pain. Thought came of Mother attempting to abort me. (I felt prolapse the past few weeks. Feels like I could lose a part of myself.) Words: I will not abort myself. I will not separate from myself – mind – split. Fear of dying all my life. I experienced and realized enfolding and taking in my Self in my mind. Healing.

---

[28] By Ernest Holmes.

I picked up heavy flour bags from the floor and twisted as I did so. I felt a pull in my back. I lifted the bags again to counter.

I am Patricia's prolapsed uterus.[29] I want to be seen and heard. I've been suffering, carrying guilt and shame for years. I need to let these feelings out into the light and give them to Christ. I want to be acknowledged and allowed my true function, my beautiful place of creation. She was ashamed of me and wanted to stop my function. I have slipped forward.[30] The KEY is TRUTH. Patricia didn't do it then and she is not doing this now. She blamed it on another then and is blaming God now. She hasn't fully realized truth. She thought women gave birth to a physical body. Woman does not create body; God does. It is Spirit clothed in flesh. Help me, oh Lord, as I embrace and transform this truth.

I've been diagnosed with a twisted pelvis. Prolapse means a detachment from spiritual wholeness – consciously with Mother – intuition, feminine womb. Life living me. I am living life.

I fell into a want of understanding of the body leaving this dimension. The body is not separate from the mind and the Spirit. Conscious mind is convinced, convicted. I slow down to catch up with my Self.

Fallen man is in want from the high estate of One. Body leaves in consciousness when finished here – Want of understanding plain as the nose on my face – by faith in one God – who created me one by God's faithfulness – not mine. Conscious awareness. IT IS SO. Body not separate from God – Womb – which birthed it – Womb

---

[29] Thoughts came. Patricia speaks as her uterus (Gestalt technique).

[30] *Slipped*: another word for unwanted pregnancy.

of creation. Nothing outside unity. I am Whole – One. No one says *no* to me. No one limits me. I am the life I live. In confusion, my authority is doubted. I AM my authority. This is SO. There is no wrong. Just falling away from KNOWING Grace – one with. I, alone, return to my Self.

WE CAN'T CONTRACT THE INFINITE, BUT WE CAN EXPAND THE FINITE: BODY ONE WITH.

Reiki with my friend Esther Kraybill: I realized my pregnancy with Donna. I misunderstood creation and birth – they are spiritual. Shame and bad girl was in my mind when prolapse came to tell me of my error in understanding. Race of women have an erroneous belief about their bodies and birth – feeling separate from creation – God – we are creation by nature. It is *impossible* to separate from God or good. Thinking we can is a misunderstanding.

I *felt* truth of Cause. Esther felt greatly expanded in Consciousness. One with all nature.

HOW CAN I NOT BE AWARE OF YOUR PRESENCE? YOU BIRTH ME ANEW EVERY MOMENT. I AM ALIVE, FOR YOUR GAZE IS CONSTANT ON ME. YOUR GAZE IS MY ETERNAL GRACE, ETERNAL PRESENCE. I AM HELD TOGETHER IN YOUR EYES – I REFLECT YOU BACK TO YOUR SELF, MY SELF. IN THIS CO– ETERNAL GAZE WE BIRTH THE HOLY SPIRIT. BY YOUR FAITHFULNESS, I ADHERE TO TRUTH, TO DIVINE LIFE NOW AND NOW EVERMORE.

On my deck from 9:00 to 11:00 p.m. The night is clear and warm. The sky spoke to me of Oneness. I know every star, every moon, every planet, and every world within worlds. Everything is part of me and I am One with it. I feel this all-inclusiveness, a band enclosing me. I live in its endless boundaries. I am known to each and every particle of life. Flowers embrace me in their fragrance. I inhale the Life, the Spirit of each one. They respond to my appreciation. The sky is in "here." I AM the stars, moons, planets, worlds, universes. Sophia's song echoed back to me. Each time reverberating in me deeper and deeper. Spirit danced in me. This body is alive. A life! Dancing with the stars.

In bed. Many faces and lights appeared to me. I felt a cool air on my forehead and nose. Softly and tenderly acknowledging my Self and Self – Me. Words of Oneness, Unity, Being adhered to perfection. Words deeply meaningful; true, purposeful, uniting. I am upheld by thy Right Hand – Righteousness – Holy – Pure – Sure Foundation. I cannot move away from this. I cannot slip out of line with. There is Absoluteness and that is All. Faithfulness. Gratefulness spilled out of me in tender sobs and tears. Promises sang songs to me and Promise received them in me. Holy, Holy Night. Interchange: "This is too much. I didn't do this." "Oh, yes, you did, and more." "Your desire to express me more perfectly and fully, forever and ever."

A pure white left hand appeared. White female faces. A group of females to my upper left, near me. My Holy Mother. "You have come. You have come – never in my thought. But you have come!!" You heard my need and came quickly, surely. They are correcting female issues of the womb. I am fully aware of this, as I am told by Holy Mother.

Then I saw a flower – fully open, center exposed and alive – movement of life. It first looked like a soft, velvet, purple cloak surrounding itself. Then the large, soft petals lay open upon themselves, revealing the life center of creation. A cool air lit once again on my forehead and nose. Then Albany family, children, came into awareness. This is for them. I pass it on. The Gift.

ADHERE TO MY GOD – MOTHER

Holy Mother, thank you for making yourself known to me, for claiming me as your own. You are here with me always.

Prolapse means a falling away from, a slipping forward.

In bed, inner excitement. Work continues. "If it doesn't do beautiful work, then it doesn't do anything." "There is nothing to this." It doesn't exist; it is not real. I realized these words: Only good and beautiful are created. Obstetrics. There can be no obstruction to right action.

"What about the second one?" – Doug. I did nothing to Doug. Nothing was done because there is no obstruction to right action. Hallelujah!! Now I KNOW THIS IS TRUE. I free Self, including Doug, who is part of All Mind. My consciousness is expanded and so is His.

How can I be conscious of what is not? This is how I became conscious of imperfection. I am conscious only of what *is*. I am cause to see only the Perfect when I understand *truth*. I am conscious only of God – Goodness, beauty, love – *I get it.*

The cause of error is error, a mistake of unreal for real. Belief in sin, bad girl – hate – that feeling.

Doug is self-esteem, self-confident, never giving up, a success.

I believe my word is the law of that where unto it is spoken. The word of truth, light. Understanding absolutely erases error (Science of the Mind).

WITHIN ME IS UNBORN POSSIBILITY OF LIMITLESS EXPERIENCE. MINE IS THE PRIVILEGE OF GIVING BIRTH TO IT.

Prolapse came. Let it go. It is just a mindset. I AM not human; I AM Divine. This body is not human. I was mistaken. I AM Divine. Words of power. I felt stuck in position. The movement of my low back was painful in changing position. "Yes, the human position is painful. You took it on, you believed your eyes and ears – lies. Believe only in Me. *I AM All.*" "Forget it." The human condition is a dream, an illusion. "Don't listen to anyone else. They don't know who I AM. They only believe what they see."

I AM growing into my Eternal Self. My spine is endless support, a firm foundation. The framework of Life – not shrinking – expanding. Shake upside down – facing in the opposite direction, I now see what was behind me, facing where I came from – beliefs, race mind.

Night notes: *I accept these eyes are now seeing clearly directly from the heart of God.*

January 22

Ed asked if my feet were cold. I said yes. I was in awareness that I was affirming what I did not want – discomfort, an accepted fact for years. I took the blanket off. I correct my thought.

While holding my precious granddaughter, Sophia, in my arms, I
was inspired with words and a tune to a lullaby: *Sophia's Song*.
Dedicated to the children of the universe.

Sophia's Song

Sleep, baby dear
Nanny is near
As you drift to Dreamland;
Heaven will be
Closer for me
Angels around you stand.

Your gentle sigh
Reaching the sky
Opens Heaven's door, dear;
Welcoming you
Starlight and dew
Rest on your soft, sweet brow.

Your eyes show me
All One can see
Light and joy forever;
Round you secure
Simple and pure
Love sings her lullaby.

Song of the night
Holding you tight
Tiptoe to the stars, dear;
Yours to explore
Ever much more
Taking them to your heart.

Wisdom of light
Peace of the night
In your eyes is wonder;
Tasting your hair
Settling there
Moonlight rests softly on you.

Lend me your light
Lend me your sight
The laughter of the rainbow;
Vapors anew
Sparkling on you
Clouds pillow your sweet head.

Catching your eye
There in the sky
Silvery beams unfolding;
Only to know
One moment's glow
Held in my arms with you.

When you awake
Sunlight will take
Stardust from your eyes, dear;
Kissing your face
Will not erase
Rainbows held in your smile.

What e'er you say
Where e'er you play
The world is made for you, dear;
Brand new each day
Happy and gay
Love takes you on its wings.

Trees sway for you
Leaves dance for you
Wind is whistling softly;
Music so clear
Sweet to your ear
Earth sings her song for you.

Please take me there
I wish to share
The splendor of the stars, dear;
I hear their song
For this I long
I will go there with you.

Sophia's Song

Patricia Roedema

♩ = 100

Sleep baby dear Nanny is Near as you drift to dream land Heaven will be

closer for me angels around you stand

New thought: Fullness – opulence – overflowing – pouring forth. How can I live this truth? Profusion.

Morning notes – One to four a.m.: "REMEMBER, WE CANNOT OBJECTIFY THAT WHICH IS NOT TRUE."

Image of Patricia. She is hiding and shooting a gun.

"You were afraid of her, you were terrified. She was your sin, and sin had found you out. You hated her and wanted to kill her. Your shame was horrific." My response: This is no longer true. I love her. I am love that conceived her. She knows that now. She thrives because of my love.

What about the middle child? "Don't confuse the issue. Stay focused."

Christ is mine. He has saved it and used it well. I am confessing. "Who is? She isn't here anymore. Where is she?"

I am rising up. The smell of my own insides meets me in the form of an olfactory memory. That smell repulsed me. Now it meets me from within for recognition and release.

Give me understanding: "We cannot objectify that which is not true." I must understand all of my beautiful Self.

What more wants out? "I AM open to allowing Truth to reveal ITSELF. I'm willing Truth; error must be seen, recognized, felt, smelled, and remembered inside to out."

I am smelling flowers deeply. They are a part of me, as I AM One with them. Inhaling their beauty and fragrance to acceptance deep within – embarrassed – Oh Holy – come forth – transform me from within. I am willing. I wait. Wash me clean in the Spirit. Wash away all fear, all hate, all memory of smell.

We can only objectify truth. We can believe otherwise, but that's against self, against truth. Impossible. The stress of lying to self builds an atmosphere of stench. We can smell a liar; sulfur – evil – associated with dead.

The fragrance of Self is beautiful – my own inside. Truth is beautiful. I am beautiful in truth in my innermost being. Spirit: This is all that IS – revealed.

Error was believed and felt as hate – fear – shame against one's true nature: Love. This cannot be. There is only True Nature – One – Love. I live. Therefore, I AM True Nature. I know this consciously. All else is error because there is No else or other. I cannot claim what is not or never was. I speak only for Self. I AM.

Fear, hate, shame is no more – is not – gone – removed forever – it never was. Never was. Relief – joy – felt in my soul. I AM saved – pure – beautiful – whole – innocent – joyful – creative – expanding life.

I am finding conscious understanding of Atonement = Salvation through contemplating word of Truth. This is Light – Enlightenment.

Image of a golden left hand. Stay with this. Follow it. Truth is golden. Understanding only truth, wiping the slate clean every day or if thought is not in line with truth. I keep a close watch on this heart of mine.

Next morning, I awoke with a feeling of grave responsibility to hurt no one. An image came to mind: a woman was standing outside a cave. "Unclean." She was a leper. I am responsible only for myself. I felt cleansed of belief of being responsible for another. As I relaxed into Truth, so did my body – muscles and spine.

In bed, my feet itched. Thought: I had eaten tomatoes – too much acid.

Night notes: "I am neutralizer. I am safety pin. I hold all things together in a closed circuit of neutral power. Not charged negative or positive."

Night notes: "I am connecter."

Night notes: A clear image of my happy, vibrant self running toward me with outstretched arms.

In the morning, I awoke feeling Donna's energy. I join her in the soft empty space of love. I feel my body relax. "Ohh" – the softest of sighs. "Beautiful." Donna was just born. I experienced the soft, mystical beauty of birth – of spiritual and physical birth. Transformation of her physical birth. I felt deep joy and radiant beauty. The feelings came to Donna also.

After Reiki, I felt energy run down my spine to the root chakra. A big, bright, white light went from the psoas muscle to my left shoulder.

Morning notes: "No one is anybody." "Why the bells?" "To influence the people they serve." "I wonder how." "A new God – so I appeared to be then." "It is better for both of us." I then see the image of a skull with black, empty eye holes. "The rules we can teach them."

Night notes: "This is the house of God." A woman's face appears in an open doorway. Behind her is deep darkness.

In the morning, I awoke feeling well. I make a new choice of life, health, and freedom to choose joy and trust. I choose faith in Love, which is God's faith in me. I am His. I know body and mind are healing – I feel this deep within. I experienced energy movement, I felt it. I *know*. A big, white, energy light moved down my spine to its base.

Morning: I am in deep meditation while my Christ Mind, Holy Spirit, conscious High Self, operates with my deep conscious awareness, reestablishing my mind to truth, forever sure and faithful to the image God begot me of – His perfect Self eternally saved and secure.

Morning meditation: Image of a man's face with a white-light nose. I feel an energy block in my upper chest. Fear of smells – of gas exhaust.

Meditation: Pain in the right side of iliac crest. I doubted healing and felt fear. I entered the Christ Mind, I rose to it and beamed up my entire body. I saw an image of my facial profile with my mouth enlightened. "I am a spokesperson for God." I will manifest the thought or word I receive with no hesitation, instantly. I felt pain in my left elbow; at age five, the index finger of my left hand had been injured in the twisting motion of a meat grinder. Holy One, bring truth to this error.

I am not to hesitate when rising to walk. I am to follow through with faith in Self and God – One. His promises are sure. His word is truth. My strength is in the Lord and the power of His Might.

Meditation: I felt shooting pains. I shot myself. Have mercy, Lord. Take them [the bullets] out. Thank you. Transform this energy of guilt felt from an unforgivable sin. I see the image of a body hanging high on a hook, coming out of water, dripping wet. "You must let yourself off the hook."

Night notes: "This needs to be restored." "Modified by the group self." "Faith in thy God to do this." I felt Reiki in my hands. Bill: "It seemed like a lot." "It is by yourself. You have help." Restore unto me the joy of thy salvation. "A deep level of consciousness." "His *might* be the perfect word." The hook is feeling obligated or responsible. I believed I could be a pure channel through which God's love would flow. A human being does not achieve perfection. There is only one perfect Being – nothing else. Only God is All in All Spirit. I have lived in an atmosphere of judgment. If one doesn't realize his lessons, all are condemned, according to Patricia's beliefs. I condemned myself in believing I must be a clear channel for God's love to flow.

All are free. "God so loved the world that He gave His only begotten Son that, whosoever believes in Him, should not perish, but have eternal life. For God did not send His Son into the world to judge the world, but that the world should be saved through Him." Movement from a hard core belief to a soft, gentle, tender transition from judgment to love; from a stressful, protective position to allowing movement. All are individual expressions of Self.

I am clothed with living flesh, the Word of God, made flesh. I am God's Being, manifested.

Evolution: Roll from one side to the other, inch by inch, teaching and learning movement – slow, effortless, allowing, intending, going with it.

Night notes: "The word he passed this week was very authoritative and conceptual."

"Turn it over to God."

Night notes: I awoke to a nightmare of horror! Coughed and felt pain in my hips. What if I get a cold in this condition? I would have to go to a nursing home because I can't get up, the pain is so bad. When I cough, I would be given drugs – pneumonia. I'd rather die, but how – from pain, pneumonia, or a heart that gives out? My heart is racing with fear, irregular beats. I have a horrific fear! I felt I was in a bind with no good choice left, nowhere to turn. A complete failure. Loss of bladder and bowel control. Shame. The next morning I had a realization: This nightmare played out of my subconscious where it had actualized as the condition experienced. My intent to turn all my fears over to God was a fresh, conscious belief and faith before falling asleep. Turn it over, this needs to be restored. The other side is release, freedom, relaxation. My body felt relaxed and movement was free of guard to pain.

Daddy's terrible, rasping cough, wracking his body before he went to the hospital. Patsy Ann slept in the same room with him and Mother. Daddy went out on a stretcher because he was too weak to walk or stand. He died.

I slept seven hours straight – the longest since the prolapse. Ed gave me Reiki on my feet before I went to sleep.

Meditation: An announcer's voice: "December 7, 1941." This was President Roosevelt's announcement of the attack on Pearl Harbor. I was lying on my back and felt a type of jump start for my heart that pushed me into the mattress then up.

Meditation: Open to truth. Patsy Ann was three years old. She picked up shock waves from her family gathered around the radio when the attack was announced. Mother held Patsy Ann on her lap. She was paralyzed with shock. When realized, truth heals. Freedom to move. Flexibility is restored and a state of gratitude to God – Christ.

Night notes: I felt discomfort in my hip muscles. Lord, where do you want me to go now? "I will pull up your nightgown." Why? "You've been gone a while." "You can see it" "Don't assume that's sexual abuse." Image: Mother's face, with her tongue licking a vagina. She couldn't have done that to me. Where do I go next, muscles (still feeling discomfort)? Roll over? "No. Go to truth – on your back." Truth is everlasting. "Be done with it."

Worked with Donna. "It says sexual to me." Patricia: Go to truth on your back. Donna and I join in meditation, allowing truth to unfold.

Patsy Ann is lying on her back across the outhouse seat. Her brother is with her, licking her vagina. I asked why he would do that. What made him think of that? Donna said, "Blow job." Did he blow the vagina? Donna says, "That's done to males. Someone did that to him." Mother. That's why Mother's face came up and

98

also why Mother and Brother came up to me in Reiki. I feel pain in my hips and back. I feel unsettled, in need of comfort.

Meditation: I experience a rising of the kundalini[31], a spiritual orgasm. Could a child have an orgasm? Donna says *yes*. The perpetrator asks, "Does it feel good?" I had an orgasm as a child. Why does the child feel ashamed and silenced? Donna says, "By the words the perp uses to protect himself: Don't tell or else... My brother said, "Or I will be punished." I loved my brother and didn't want him to get hurt.

Revelation: I have felt a morbid sense of responsibility for the children on my watch. I have *always* felt a fear of them getting hurt, a terrible and unrealistic weight.

I want closure and comfort.

Meditation: I realize the blessedness of life and healing. I freed my mother's family line at an earlier time and now I free my brother. What an honor to be part of it. I'm feeling deep compassion for all human beings and am grateful to be part of it all. I feel joyful and awed.

I felt awareness of my sexual body and vagina: It was frozen and lacked sensitivity of touch – needed reclaiming to be whole – in all my parts. The weight of responsibility of no harm to my grandchildren broke down the rigidity of the pelvic girdle and brought back feeling – fear of someone on my charge getting hurt. I must know truth. Pain is illusion, error, lie. Turn it over to God –

---

[31] A form of primal energy that may awaken in deep meditation and lead to enlightenment and bliss.

good – to clear the channel. *This was the cleared channel that was my earliest desire – the birth canal – creativity. Now realized.*

Night notes: "I am the Light." I was awake in awareness of this thought all night.

I realize more deeply. Outer conditions are brought up to the inner word, Spirit – Answer. The awareness of mind to accept and embrace, enfold, obtain. The Father greets me with outstretched hands. Every moment the field of Mind is ready to accept and bring to manifestation my thought. The light is wherever we go. We can't be out of the light. We simply turn to it and no longer see a shadow or illusion. I feel I am in a cocoon of life, safe and secure.

January 25

Realizing more deeply. I am limitless. Life runs over with good all the time. I don't wait for it; I accept it and claim it. I think big and bigger. My word is invincible. I feel this in a cocoon. Life supplies all my needs.

The law regarding an eye for an eye, tooth for a tooth is not a punishment; it does not take anything from us. It mirrors exactly what I accept and receive. The alpha and omega, beginning and end, are the same. The beginning of thought is the end of thought. Instant. It is, and it works, every second. This is a new realization.

These words came during a moment of tender, loving awareness while sitting with the family at the dinner table.

There is my son, sitting between his girls
Polished to a soft luster, not too much, just right.
There are moments in between heartbeats
When one seems to slip into a crack in the floor.

January 27

Morning words: Awoke to "I have a block." Answer: There can be no block. I AM light; I AM all good; I AM clear mind. I see clearly light – everywhere.

Later, I saw an image of a bald spot on the back of a man's head. A fear thought – that it was an image in my mind. I will let go of it. It remained persistent. I was trying of myself, unsuccessfully, until I asked for help. Answer: There is no empty space. All is mind and spirit – alive and becoming at all times and in all places.

Morning meditation: "He adores[32] you." I adore my Self. The Christ Mind adores me. How precious.

February 4

Meditation: I am opening to a greater acceptance of all that is. There is lots of energy movement. I saw a child's face and heard, "I made a mess." I felt shaking and unsettled for a few brief moments. Lots of bright, clear, green energy forms appear. I

---

[32] *Adore*: To honor as a deity or as divine; regard with reverent admiration and devotion.

accepted healing after I let go of fear and anxiety. *I know I am whole.* I felt soft and firm. A fabric appeared. It was heather blue and white.

February 5

I awoke with a mental awareness of Holy One showing me something for my understanding. Words: "Consider Peter's place."[33] I remember Mother's experience with a fallen bladder. She said it felt like a penis. While doing work around my birth, I realized I felt uncomfortable around handicapped people. I couldn't look at them. I had taken on my parents' judgment of me. I was not enough. I had no penis. Women are not as good as men. Only men had rights. Women didn't count. The Holy One's words "Consider Peter's place" came with an intense feeling of physical restlessness. I was unable to be still, so I allowed my restlessness to express itself. It had to be acknowledged and affirmed. I did not know until this point in time how much I have held unsettled and not accepting of being a physical woman. I had cold feet and nothing below the pelvis. A physical feeling of protrusion these past few weeks brought my attention to being female again. Also awareness that claiming "my feet are cold" affirmed a lack of life. I had disclaimed my extremities. I needed to be aware of the feeling of discomfort (i.e., "Consider Peter's place") my mind had just created – Confusion. I could not understand as an infant. I now understand and accept myself completely woman (I had a question about how to balance hormones, and it has been answered.) I knew it was possible. I am instantly whole.

---

[33] Peter: name chosen for Patricia had she been a boy.

February 6

Awoke to viewing a newly formed fetus in a womb, possibly two. The vision changed to a fully birthed baby lying in what appears to be a nest of energy. Birth of new idea, manifestation of new thought, new growth, One from two.

February 7

On waking, I heard my grandson James's voice say, "You want it that badly that you're going to take it?" Yes! I felt I had taken it (that is, accepted it) with the response. It is mine. Done unto me. I possess it for use in Spirit.

Night notes: *I PERCEIVE THAT, BECAUSE I AM A SON OF GOD, BECAUSE OF THIS INFINITE THING THAT OVERSHADOWS ETERNITY AND FINDS ITS ABIDING PLACE IN ME, I KNOW THAT ALL GOOD IS MINE NOW.*

Only good and loving kindness shall follow me all the days of my life and I will dwell in the house of the Lord forever. I have reached a high mark in Mind and Spirit. I accept, allow, affirm, and permit its outward manifestation in my material world and affairs. Perfect Life, Perfect Healing, Perfect Harmony, Divine Guidance, Infinite Strength, Joy – Forever. I AM peaceful, poised (inner calm). My mind rests in realization of Mind is All. This is Power. Infinite. I felt a release in my tailbone area.

Night notes: "I need your help." "I will help. I say *yes* to all that is asked of me." "I can do anything with my helper."

Night notes: Image: A right hand is extended to me. I put my left hand in it. I feel light – joyful. Invitation to dance. My Holy

Partner leads and I follow as One. I saw physical brown eyes –
clear – large – whites – white.

Night notes: "What can I do for you?" You welcome and embrace
me. I feel our Oneness, your love for me, and mine for you. These
moments are Holy Communion. "What can I do for you, my
love?" "Have faith in me." "I do have faith in you (me). You are
my love." (I feel both voices are mine.) There is only One voice.
"What can I give you, dear One?" "Stand still on this very sight,
this exact sight, this very same sight." "Oh, yes! I *hear*. I *see*. I *know*.
I *am*." My spirit swoons.

BELIEFS ARE NOT POWER, ONLY AGGRESSIVE SUGGESTION.
My consciousness is life-preserving; pure, clear, Holy. In God's
universe there is no error, mistake, or lack. There is only endless
Good, Life, Harmony, Spirit manifesting Self.

The ever-present Spirit of God lifts me to Universal Consciousness
– Grace, in which is one condition: perfection.

My understanding is grounded in realization of Omnipresence.
All needs are met through Grace.

I am convicted and confident with unfolding good. I live by
Grace.

I am the light of the world. There is no darkness. Grace is the Self
of you and me.

Meditation: "Much happiness to you in your new home."

Night notes: Male voice: "Have you ever seen a more beautiful
twenty-year-old in all your life?"

I awoke to warm, soft, gentle feelings within. A deeper, greater awareness of completeness, purity, power of Love and Life, I AM. I AM inspired to fullness of manifestation in honor of this Self. I AM guided beautifully and gloriously. I AM carried through this transition in heavenly Grace.

Night notes: *Harmony is the only and ever-present state of being.*

Consider not the things of this world. I tune into the beam that leads to realization of "My Kingdom."

In this consciousness are riches of the soul, palaces of spiritual substance, House of God – existence of Eternal Bliss. I trust my instinct, my intuition.

My infinite good unfolds without taking thought; as person, place, and thing is really God, Good, Life expressing, Love revealing Gifts (Holy Spirit) of God. Divine Grace – my heritage as a child of God.

I swoon in Grace, overwhelmed by your Love.

The kingdom of God appears as you and me. Truth reveals more of God to the world. Illusion is my concept of the manifestation of God, a belief it has power to harm. Illusion misinterprets reality itself. It is not "out there." I have no right to condemn myself or another. I do not accept worldly beliefs. I am not growing healthier or perfect. I am perfect expression *now*.

When I AM voices itself to me, human selfhood disappears.

Our humanhood must not be exalted into thinking it is God. Where desire is, manifestation must be. The Lord gives me the desire of my heart. His word is truth and sure. Help! Insight me, my Consciousness, my intuition with Holy desire. Healing is in order. I am done with physical health, supply of a physical nature, or material sense of good.

My purpose is realization of spiritual sense of existence: only continuity of good endlessly.

Healing is offered and accepted through Grace. Love with a smile. My mind governs and controls all my affairs. I am the Captain of my soul, the Master of my destiny.

Experience: I desired to be close to my true self: Christ.[34] Lots of energy patterns appeared and then a face presence that drew me into itself.

Night notes: Inner awakening. I saw puffy cloud-like patterns. "I bless you in all you do and see." "I am Life and Love in you." "All current" (energy). "What if I don't see him again?" Male voice: "Will you join me, my love?"[35]

"I'll be giving Reiki initiation in Spirit." "I am spiritualized in all." "He is a direct implant." "Okay." Messiah, "Did you hear me? Did you hear me?" I needed to write all this down and did so after second command.

IMPLANTED IN MY CONSCIOUSNESS – GOD.

---

[34] Patricia's true self.

[35] *Join*, as in connect as a live wire through will or desire.

"Will you rise with me?" "Of course I will. I always have." "You are just getting used to knowing it." "You cannot move without me." "You are within me and I in you. Remember?" "I am Life. All Life."

Realization: I have everything within me. I am everything. There is only One Life, God, Consciousness. God not only gives Life; He is the Life He gives.

Meditation: I am joining you. I will connect to your energy consciously through my intent. You are the desire of my heart, my love, to beat as one, to feel your presence. I heard piano chords playing strong harmony – music. "Time to take the heat out of those pockets" (i.e., tone the energy down). I felt pulsing in root and crown chakra. "Last night He took me out to the house where Patricia had been."

NATURE OF ERROR CLAIMS TO OPERATE – IT CLAIMS ONE'S IDENTITY, POSSESSES ONE, TAKES ONE OVER. (WE REFER TO THIS NATURE AS EGO.)

I awoke to an inner voice: "You are perfect. I am perfect in you." I felt presence of life, tingling energy throughout my body. I felt light, exquisite. I turned onto my side. My body felt deeply relaxed. I felt a release in my neck; my entire body was soft. I sat up on the side of the bed, taking this all in. I am NOW new. All nature bows to me. All life honoring, blessing, and serving me. Life brings joy and beauty, gratitude overflows my heart for my creator – omnipotent God, omnipresent, omniscient is sacred trust, to glorify and manifest the heart of Love. Grace abounds.

MESSIAH IS MY OWN DIVINE IDEA OF GOD. I AM MY OWN MESSIAH, ONE IN, AND WITH. THE STILL, SMALL VOICE CONFIRMED IT LAST NIGHT. "I AM PERFECT IN YOU. YOU ARE PERFECT."

Night notes: "Happy birthday to you." "I've got to drive to the devil for this" (Where did that come from!). "Understand, this was six years ago."[36]

"I am the highest Consciousness God. I am Spirit. I am truth. I am all there is. No voice but mine to listen to." I could have swooped up right over you, Lord. I believed I could have. "No such thing." We are one, not two. I am forever *now* – there is no past, no future. The Lord God established me eternally, forever. I am the Lord thy God. Thou shalt have no other Gods before me.

"Amusement park. No amusement park. You have no place for one. Get away, get away. You still don't really get away. There is no place to go. Think. Where are you sending me? Who am I? What are you trying to get rid of? Truth transforms. There is nothing in me that is enemy to my Self. There is only Life and Truth. There is nothing to hide from or fear. All is good. Only good exists. No one has ever bowed the knee to evil. There is one power only: God, Life, Good." "Thank you, Truth evermore."

Praise God. "How was your date?" Joyful. "You are going to a wonderful closet." The secret place of the most High God – Messiah.

---

[36] Patricia was tempted to believe in a false god.

Awoke to my internal voice. "You do not appreciate me." I am not appreciating my Spirit, not relying on Spirit – trusting. There is only one voice. Thank you, Holy One.

"Hip to hip." My inner voice. One. There is only one voice. He cannot leave me. I can never leave Him. Realization: I never did!

Meditation: I desire to appreciate you, my Savior, Lord, and King. How can I show this? "Not empty words. Believe in me. Action." I've not been doing stairs or bending. Lord, you must lead me. I can do nothing of myself. After contemplating this, I hear what I've been doing in the words I speak. Out of habit, I speak to God as a person "out there," a separate power.

I have received realization and understanding of my spiritual self. There is no other God or power. I am God in physical manifestation as mind, soul, body, One. I was cheating myself of the Divine Birthright my Messiah implanted in me.

Understanding is action; thought is power. My muscles have been holding me safe until I accept my Self. Thank you, Patricia, Holy One.

Night notes: "There is a good part of this that I'm just going to give you."

Treating myself like a precious object will make me strong. Cherishing Self gives me strength.

I received Reiki from my friend, Barbara Gascho. I shook for an hour, afraid to let go, that a muscle would pull. My body needed to let go of all fear and stored tension of hurting another and of feeling responsible for their happiness. I shed tears of relief.

Esther Kraybill sent Reiki: I saw an image of a tiger face. I was also focused on the words "Be still and know I am God." She felt the wind on the water – Moses at the Red Sea that had parted and held back. I am crossing the Red Sea. Yes. I felt affirmation. I come through to Truth – all goodness, the land of milk and honey. The tiger face – new adventure – awakening of power and passion within life.

Night notes: Image: A young woman with her left arm outstretched, strong, powerful voice – beautiful from within. A blanket of the universe descended upon me: Stars were shining, lights were aglow over my abdomen, fire of Holy was upon me. I was preserved (i.e., frozen). I'm now being restored in conscious awareness, testifying to truth. Voice of power, High Self resounding on my instrument, chords like strings vibrate to call of life.

Night notes: "I am reviving." "I am recovering." "I am sensitive and fragile."

No comfortable position of peace and quiet in bed. God is not one side or the other. God is All. Aware of a tight place in a muscle on my side. Fear! Pneumonia? A morbid picture of death came up: Daddy's death. This is the next issue to deal with. Fear must be faced, looked at. All must be done in order. Fear of Life – hurt another – a lie!

Meditation: Twelfth chakra is opening one inch right to the center of my head – ignited, sparked, living light – understanding. I am light bearer into darkness – fear. I am experiencing physically, expanding Consciousness as my mind, body, and soul are restored. All needs to be understood and known. I felt a tightness in my right shoulder release. The tightness had been the "holding of a position" to avoid movement – pain, or stretching. A yielding. I heard, "Never. No, never." I consciously said, "Always. Yes, always." I remembered smelling perfume from a supermarket bag that contained fruit. I don't want perfume on my food; it's not good. I consciously affirmed all is good. We are in a process of learning and evolving back to God. All is good. A belief in error or wrong. I make my world and am a universe unto myself – self–contained, under guidance, and held by Christ Mind.

Donna and Esther give me Reiki. Esther sees two UPS trucks (representing delivery, comfort, completion). Two planes (dimensions) tugging me in a gold room with three birds, ladies dancing in colorful costumes, a light shining from this gold room inside a stone temple. There is a silk curtain, a dog barking, a bath or pool on a hill, Jack's swayback, the horse that threw Jack off. The secret was out about Mother and Jack – and also about Donna!

My uterus wanted to talk. It revealed that Jack's back caused him great pain. I took the voice of my pain and realized there's a misbelief that pain returns to you if you think or speak about it. My uterus is free of holding pain and shame. (From an earlier visit with Barbara, when she used a twisting motion, I felt faint as a result.) There are bright, moving blobs of color and light. Straightening out my thinking straightens out my spine and pelvis to align. To focus on Truth of Perfection casts out fear. I ask if anything is left to be revealed about my experience. I see lights on Donna's eyes, cheek, hands, and above her head. Raised awareness and Consciousness of all life coinciding with our rising to new heights, as ushered in by a mountain goat – with its flexible skeleton and strong, gripping feet and legs – up, up! With precise aim and accuracy, then surefootedness when leaping to a small, seemingly dangerous, place.

I feel completion regarding the experience with my back. Blue Christmas lights from my mother's house windows prompted us to lift her up. She was diving and swooping, dancing and flying – flexibly and joyfully! Donna asked for clarity of mind and vision for her son, Joe, in learning about body and health in medical school. There is laughter, lights; my head is open – open-mindedness. I have a good, happy feeling about myself. More lights and colors appear – blobs of color moving and growing. Energy waves from the right. Purple and green circles move into the center. Donna said it was a good idea for her story of twin healings.

Reiki with Donna: Feel I am the center of the universe: suspended, weightless – straighten out Mind and body. Image: a heart and shadows of people walking. Two of the Three Stooges. I have invited the joy of my salvation; lighten up and choose to see humor. Myrtle Peterson.[37] Legs like pipes with large shoes at the ends – muscle disorder – a prehistoric mastodon in water using its front legs to pull itself out onto land. Its back legs are crippled and the animal stumbles out. Flash to the hind legs.

"Release her from bondage in your mind." I am to set Myrtle free from the image I hold of her in my mind. I put her on the altar to turn her over to God. As I did so, other crippled or deformed people from my childhood came to mind: Margaret Krause, farm

---

[37] Patricia's farm neighbor. In life, Myrtle was crippled.

neighbor, had rheumatoid arthritis; my cousin George Zimmerman, had a brain injury from birth; Jack Smith, my mother's friend, whose spine had been crushed in an accident. Saint John was present when Jack came to mind. Jack sat up and walked away from the altar. I felt great joy. These neighbors, my cousin, and Jack were my early childhood impressions of deformity.

Reiki with Esther: I was paralyzed with fear and confusion at the sight of crippled people. My mind and body need straightening out. See all as whole and perfect, including myself. In the very place where pain *seems* to be, the presence of God IS. Illusion; there is no space or pressure in Reality. Mind is corrected. Only God, Spirit, energy is real.

Pain sitting on my right butt. The top and bottom don't fit together. I felt great pressure on my sacroiliac joint. The pressure went right into my arms, especially the right one. I felt alone and scared. Ed slept in my room. He supported my arm when I went to the bathroom. I was having spasms.

I called Donna for Reiki and slept for several hours, till I awoke from a dream: two figures in the dark – I knew them to be Ed and his sister, Marilyn. They were reclining and kissing. His mother and two of his sisters were sitting next to her. They were all outside the house. Marilyn sat behind her mom. I said, "I saw the whole thing. Don't act like you don't know. Marilyn knows and it's your fault, Mom." I told Ed my dream and my realization of what it meant. On awakening, I remembered a great emotional injury I had experienced thirty years prior involving Ed. We were at his big office Christmas party. Ed was drunk and dancing with a woman from his office. He was falling all over her, making love on the floor. I sat and watched – stunned, humiliated, in total disbelief. The incident was never brought up. I asked him how he felt about the pain I was in. He said, "In your mind, you saw—" I said, "Oh, no! You *did* this!" He couldn't remember – didn't want to remember. I felt I needed his verification to feel justified in my pain and anger. I was over–the–top upset and took it to my Superior Mother. I asked, "How can I let go of this anger? I need to understand."

He did the best he could with his life and I did the best I could with mine. I had erroneous beliefs and thinking, as did he. We both brought our respective baggage into our union and did the best we could. I am free. Ed is free. We are responsible only for our own choices and pain.

After that realization, I slept well. When I next awoke, I lay in bed, grateful for movement. I sat on the bed. I am sitting at the right hand of the Father. I am His action, His manifestation. I am freedom of movement. As His daughter, I am in Him, He is in me. We are *not* separate. I feel into Self and acknowledge God consciously as all. I walk slowly in awareness.

I sat to read with Ed and pain came into my left leg. Ed gave me Reiki on my feet. What is this pain saying? To be open to the revelation of Truth. A remnant of fear remains in my subconscious: at death, there is a return to the universal subconscious mind of God – a vain regret to lose built-up errors and illusions (i.e., the ego body) of the conscious mind. This is the silliest and most illusory fear of all mankind and one of the strongest. Ego does not want to die. We retain all aspects of Self, the good we have acquired. All is God acting through us and only good exists in reality. It can never be lost. Truth is everlasting. Knowledge of truth embraces all mankind. Give freely, for freely I have been given. Be done with it! Pain, error – all is truth when understood!

Night notes: "I am realizing the fiber of my being, consciously." "This is nice." "I am taking care of it." "For the sex orientation."

Image: I opened the basement.

Night notes: I moved my leg and the doctor said, "Good." "I am wholly good." "You are a prostitute." "Lie. I deny that as not true." "Into the gambling of the balance."

My daughter was with me in my fear of labor. My daughter was with me in my fear being revealed in Reiki and was holding my hand.

Bicycle – me – conscious and subconscious fused together. Donna remembered dog attack on bike and our fear.[38]

"When they fell off the trike." When? "To them." Donna fell off her tricycle when she was six years old. "Something worse will come upon you," from the Bible. It was misunderstood and caused fear. "I know. Ha, ha." "You heard it. Yes, yes." "Speaking it out disputes it."

Reiki with Donna: Revealing of cause and truth. I was very uneasy. Did not feel centered. I remembered spanking Donna when she threw tantrums. I was afraid of being evicted from our apartment. The landlord slept days. I carried guilt. I was a bad

---

[38] A car came along, struck and killed the dog.

mother and I felt ashamed. I turn myself and her over to you, Lord. Have mercy on her that she may have Truth revealed to her. I experienced an energy pattern, and flashes of light evolve in my mind. "It was just like that, that you could find the way." Peace. I felt great relief and gratitude. It was you all the time, Lord.

Meditation: Friendship with Holy Spirit – Forever Friend – Ed is sitting in his chair. I asked to hear vibration of love. Ed handed me a small TV control and said, "Here – Hear." It is a monotone. One morning I will wake up and feel fine. I will have forgotten the feeling of pain or caution (caution gave credence to pain) and will remember only who I AM.

Give me the tone. I am awake.

"READY, SET, GO."

I AM traveling back with you, feeling in a familiar place. I AM remembering Self. In mind's eye, I see a window and green grass growing outside. I see new growth. I witness myself walk barefoot in new grass. I FEEL life. Back is behind me; my past is healed. Surely Goodness and Mercy follow me all the days of my Life and I shall Live in the House of the Lord FOREVER. *KNOW His Family NOW.* We are One. We will go over the hill together, one step at a time, effortlessly.

Feel this space. *Oh, ah, ah, ah, ah, lay, lu, jah,* unto Christ our Heavenly King. *Allelujah.* Up from the grave He arose. Christ is living truth; nothing is solid. ALL IS spirit manifesting. "Did He furnish it with all new furniture?" "Yes. All NEW." I FEEL

FAITH. I FEEL Confidence of life. Life comes to me in feeling and thought.

Life is living me more consciously today. My thought is deeply anchored in Trust of Life. My thought lives in this body as energy and power, One with ITSELF, expressing and receiving its Great One Being in me TODAY more fully than ever. Life as thought IS FAITH in Good, in All Love, Harmony, Joy, and Beauty.

Today I inhale this love which I AM as One Anointed as I AM. I move into this Space of Love. I expand; I express this Love in Beauty – manifested to glorify Glory in the flesh. This space is peace. I behold the Father Self as Faithful Life. In this space, the monotone, perfect harmony is felt and heard from energy and thought power. ONE TRUTH IS. I AM THIS.

Grace abounds; I live into the Space – Grace – given freely ALL I intend to behold. ALL IS MINE TODAY. I REJOICE and AM GLAD. I AM this DAY. Here I am, coming to my Self for heartfelt love, my daily bread as my heart feels empty, I come to live in the Space of All. My thought leads me here with my love.

What can I do? I stand corrected. What can the Holy do for me? Listen! With my heart. The House of God declares its Word this day. This is my Father's World and, to my listening ears, all nature sings and round me clings the music of the spheres.

I hear the Holy Word throughout this temple, deep into the Altar, Sacred (sacroiliac) Space of my being. I am raised in Christ Mind to Heavenly Place, Seated at the Right hand of God, Life, Good, Love. I Rest in Righteousness, Right thoughts. This day I rest,

KNOWING Word of Truth is vibrating throughout the World. Thy Will Be Done. SO IT IS.

I sit today, my Lord, peacefully at your right hand. Tears of gratitude and joy overflow. A quiet body, a quiet heart, are mine. It is done. Thy Will is done on earth as in Heaven. I settle into the softness of Eternal Love. I feel One with this Love. I AM Love. I AM Harmony and joy singing from my Soul. I AM kindness and compassion flowing forth from the river within.

I awoke at night to feeling two places in my abdomen. My uterus is now attached.

Speak, Holy One, from the deep place in sciatica that has something to say when pressed on. I believe I will forget God without pain. Fear – old ancient belief – not true. *I KNOW GOD.* I remember God forever and ever. Seal this truth to my heart. "I will."

Meditation with Donna: An image comes of me in the driver's seat. "I can do it." "Don't do it."

Night notes: "I AM full of Grace." This is my heritage as a child of God.

Donna received a message similar to mine as well as a vibration of harmony. Harmony is in tune with the Infinite. Hope and expectancy are vibrations in tune with all good. I had been fearing vibration of nerves – an error. Fear is always error. God is here. God is all good. I am God expressing individually in manifestation, in the unfoldment of our awareness of Spiritual

118

Truth and Light. All God, my very Consciousness is, I Am. I am not necessary to anyone's demonstration of life. I let go all personal sense of knowing.

Night notes: Seeking to realize God Consciousness is an illusion. Realization of the Kingdom of Heaven.

Meditation: "I AM here where you are. My Spirit lifts you." Image: A woman touching the robe of Jesus. She reached out and took hold of it. She knew she would be healed. I recently had an image of the bottom of His robe passing by me. I did not reach out. I must take hold of my healing in faith and know it is done unto me.

"It is I." I am on my knees before the Lord. I see only His right hand. "Touch my hand. I am real." I swooned and collapsed on my knees (not able to bend since muscle collapse). Then I was prostrate before Him (I cannot lie flat on stomach since injury). Then I am looking down from above at a limp cloak where I had lain. This is an out-of-body experience. The reality of my Savior, my resurrected Lord, raised me above the illusion of the physical senses of the world. I "felt" and "saw" the nothingness of the world's powerlessness.

"I will never leave you nor forsake you. Remember me." The Lord is with Thee. Blessed art Thou among women and blessed is the fruit of your womb, Jesus. This whereon you stand is holy ground (Bible). I am raised with Christ. Praise God! I am given dominion over the things of the earth and the thoughts above (mental realm). Neither things nor thoughts govern, control, or affect me. Spiritual Consciousness is all present.

Meditation: The illusion of error never happened. I have been forever sealed in faith and trust in my Father. It's impossible to betray that trust. "I am Prince of Peace. I have come that you may have life abundant" – now we know its fullness. Praise to the Source of all life. I pour out my heart of love to you. (I felt discomfort.) You are my comfort, Lord, and my peace. Sense is an illusion. I hold on to Truth! What appears as evil or lack is an aggressive mental suggestion and, with this realization, error destroys itself, has no power.

Night notes vision: Human left eye – old – Eye of the ages. Vibrations, colors, scale, chakras. This day is new. I allow it to unfold.

I am awakened by the sound of a boom. Breaking of a sound barrier.

Morning notes and image: Several music notes. New thought is creative. Heard deep sounds like music, a voice – vibration – on slow speed. I heard notes: D, B-flat, D, F, A-flat, B-flat – as a chord. A new chord evolving. Music of the spheres.

I am an instrument of Life. Life is a choice – playing tune of the moment. Vibration is affected only by Cause – Source. How we perceive emotion as energy movement is awareness to thought. Purpose of life is immediate, continuously in change. Effort is our intention. One hundred percent is ideal – NOW. *LOVE IS IN AWARENESS OF WHAT WE ARE THINKING AND DOING.*

*EVERYTHING, EVERY MOMENT, MATTERS AND IS WORTH
ALL OUR LIFE. LOVE, DIVINITY IS NOT SEPARATE. ALL IS
DIVINE, HOLY.*

Meditation: Realization: *Everything I experienced in the past is Holy
Divine Love only, touching me. There is One Mind, and this Mind is
God – Source. Each human is individual expression of God Mind. Each
unfolds from within itself completely as truth and Life. Each is Holy. I
AM Holy. Error is nothing; it does not exist. Only God IS.*

Awoke to: "Now we have real healing." I am complete in God, my
Self. Ed's voice: "To when I first beheld you from the heart of
God."

Night notes: "Not on doctor's schedule of exercise." "Now we
experience real belief in Self."

Night notes: "Hey, little girl. Good to see you." Doctor at my
birth. Deep purple.

Meditation: God is my Consciousness unfolding mind, body,
Spirit, One – not *as* manifestation, but *is* – Not separate.
Realization IS body manifesting.

Meditation: Feeling of gratefulness to unfolding Consciousness.
Feeling within Life; Power expressing as individual body, mind,
spirit. I AM this Life.

Belief is not a cause. I, the high self of me, the Messiah Savior in
my Consciousness – Mind is the only Cause – God – Source. Error
is dispelled in this realization.

Vision: Mystical experience. *Jesus came to my bed, knelt down facing
my head, and extended His right hand to my abdomen.* Before He came,

I had a very clear dream. I was standing inside the entrance of a church with a man and a woman. Mary spoke clearly and authoritatively on a subject which I intuitively affirmed and witnessed as true. I *felt* it inside me.

Jesus wore a long-sleeved, natural gray, tweed tunic top and pants. He had a close beard and His hair was trimmed to the head. This actually occurred in my bedroom, at my bed. I forever see this experience and I AM this experience. *It is in me. Holy can touch only holy. We are already holy, saved before the foundation of the world.*

On waking with closed eyes, I saw a light shining on the ground directly in front of me on my path for my next step.

Meditation: Face of Christ appeared.

Upon waking: "I could have killed myself." I was tempted to believe it. "You really believed you almost killed yourself."

Night apparition: The walls of the bedroom were horizontal white wood. A waterfall, not high, created a wide stream on the left side of the room. This seemed to be actual, real. My bedroom had been transformed. This lasted for the night and felt eternal.

After meditation, a great white light flooded the room.

Night notes: "I broke up the timing with eternity." "The timing was off." "This you thought." "I am now perfect timing." "I am a thought fully unknown to God." "I listen to you, Lord (body). Why, when you kill?"

"I am the master here (mind[39])?" "One voice only. There is no death." "I believe I am this Christian conversion." "It would *really* help for the two of you to be, *feel* One, to feel I AM One." I felt an inner voice rise in me. "I need nothing." I awoke with a total feeling of pure joy.

Before sleep, I sobbed for hours in pure joy. I am Feeling One and Gratitude for my Divine Life. "Open your hand and I will give you all I can give." I felt an inner explosion of power. I need nothing. I am all.

TO LIVE IS TO BE SLOWLY BORN ETERNALLY.

Vision: When I awoke, I saw a motherly figure kneeling at my left side. Mary.

Meditation: Vision – Jesus held my head and kissed my forehead. I had dark, curly hair and was a male.

"YOU ARE MY MUSIC WHILE MY INSTRUMENT WAS SILENT."

"I'm giving you an apparition. Do what you like. Eat your peanuts. *REMEMBER YOU ARE WELL.*"

Meditation: "If you go one way, there is a stream of living waters."

Realized my great selfishness and sinfulness.

---

[39] Patricia listens to the Lord with what her body says, feels, expresses. The mind is the Lord; the body responds to the mind.

I deserve all pain. I do not deserve to be healed. I have been a hypocrite. I judged all people. I judged God. I used gifts and felt self–glorified. I believed I was special, wonderful, greatly loved. I believed I had the tiger by the tail. I believed in sin. I am a mass of rotting humanity.

After this realization, I was in a state of deep remorse, followed by hopeless despair. I asked, "So where am I now?" I am free to relax and enjoy the journey. The whole of life is in the hands of the Almighty. I am more and more deeply realizing my oneness with all humanity and God's *Allness* in me and in everyone. I feel humor and lighthearted, relaxed.

I know I am saved and sealed in absolute truth.

Night notes: "It says you don't trust you, Lord."

Vision: Alyssa and I were comparing two things. Mine was a large structure with a small piece on the bottom of it. Hers was a small piece identical to mine, but without a structure.

Words come: "You seem small compared to me." "How can I trust you? I want." "It's not a matter of reason. It's of Will." "I will trust you, Lord." "I am your trust. You do nothing. I do all. I give you trust. Trust is of me. All is mine. All is of me. Of yourself, you have nothing to give." "Yes, Lord. I wait on the Lord." "Remember when I have kept you from destruction. I have never allowed you to go hungry or without."

I awaken to realizing Supernatural Power of Body.

Meditation: Today I realize truth in spirit body. "This will hurt." "No." I am expanding goodness – growing, building, developing greater and greater eternally. Purple (inner vision) bursts of pure white sparkling, expanding light (understanding). A tree as a sapling can grow around obstacles as it reaches more light. Seal this truth to my heart, Lord. "What is done is done."

Heard notes D, G, D, E – chime as harmony.

Meditation: Lord, reveal Thy Self that I may feel your presence. "You have already. That's how all this healing has taken place." "Help me to feel comfortable sitting." "I cannot help you feel comfortable physically. I am not physical." I am not feeling comfortable (relaxing or trusting), relying on your support to me to be my strength at every point. Discomfort continued until I realized I AM Consciousness. I receive truth in thought.

God is right here where I am. I am cause, not effect. There is no other cause, Only One. I am ageless – not effect of mortal mind. Until I accepted and realized this truth, I felt weightless, placeless, light. I felt turned. That's what I sought. I was answered in consciousness, in awareness of my identity. I experienced a new position as I AM Consciousness. I am instrument of Divine Intelligence. I am imbued with intelligence, wisdom, guidance, protection, gentleness, and safety for the harmonious development of my existence – all found in this Consciousness which I AM.

I travel up and down this body. Where am I? Who am I? What am I? I is God. Realize there is no room for God, Infinite Being, and anybody else besides. All that the Father has is mine. All that is true of God is true of the Son. There are no human beings. God is the only Infinite Being. I was tricked by: What about my body that is not responding. "We do not have a body." I am awakening more to my true identity.

Night notes: "Are your affairs in order?" Financial affairs? "Are the affairs of your heart and soul in order?" I am the Lord thy God. Thou shalt have no other Gods before me. I believe in one God, the Father Almighty. I am all power. I am Infinite good. Faith is active, moving, increasing infinitely.

Belief: I am all alone in this world. Told we come in alone and we leave alone – belief in birth and death. A song sang out of me: "I love you, I love you, I love you with all my heart." "I want you to realize and understand my love." Clear lights burst; purple surrounded with a gold ring of energy.

Meditation: It is God's faith in Omnipotent power of His Consciousness in me in which I am living. His Consciousness is Life. I am individual life expressing. His faith is in His Self, God which I am as His beloved son forever.

It is time to activate this faith. I am a living faith. Set this wondrous spirit free to move and express life – goodness – to manifest life. Am I in order with my Father, my Soul? "Possess ye your souls." I understand my soul is my possession. It is mine. God is mine, One Soul, One Faith, One Birth. My body is mine. My body belongs to me. Infinity flows through me as a clear channel of Consciousness, Infinite good. As I am more aware of my good, it multiplies. Aware in gratefulness. Consciousness multiplies Infinitely. Glory be to God, the Father, Son, and Holy Spirit.

Meditation: Be still and know I AM God. I AM Heavenly Host, God – One in, with, and through. My power is Love, Life, Goodness – multiplied Infinitely. I AM Super Natural Bread of Heaven. I AM established by God. I AM God's establishment. I AM His Kingdom come on earth. I AM established in Truth, God – Allness. I AM unchanging. I AM ageless. My affairs are in order.

I CONSCIOUSLY REALIZE AND UNDERSTAND WHO AND WHAT I AM IN GOD.

Night notes: "Crystal clear glass." My Consciousness is established in the Kingdom. I turned to my right side. I relax in God. Felt and heard movement that lifted my body and moved it slightly onto my back. A second sound and movement; it happened again. I got up with ease and had no discomfort walking. I adjusted my back slightly and sat comfortably without a pillow. I lifted a full glass with no strain on my back muscles.

My Consciousness appears in all forms of health and harmony for myself and others; we are One. The power of God, energy increases itself infinitely. I rest in truth. I can trust God to fulfill ITSELF. I am the book of Life.

Night notes: A thought came: Am I eating enough vegetables? Doubts and fears come forth to truth.

Meditation: "You are doing all things through me. You are always feeling my power, Love as kindness and gentleness. Always." I am a servant. The Lord is my authority. I am the Son forever. "Listen only to me." My head felt full of life. "Use your head. You shall handle vipers and not be harmed." Fear is poison to the mind. All is good. I choose the highest quality of vibration: beauty, harmony, peace, truth. I am all good, Spirit. My body is fed Super Natural Bread of Heaven. "I am cause – only cause – all good – all for you – the kingdom of Heaven. I have prepared this table before you. Prepare not for tomorrow. Allow a new day to unfold."

Jesus Christ my Savior is restoring my Soul, building Solomon's temple, the house of God, this body. I asked and He is the answer to His own desire of my heart. I am unfolding Truth, Beauty, Peace, Harmony, Joy.

Meditation: I spoke and heard Spirit say, "In the morning, I come to you." I feel full and overflowing with joy.

Night notes: "You can't talk right now?" "No, but, Rose, there's going to be happiness all over this world. He asked me to marry Him." I awoke to "Hello."

Realized the words of the 23rd Psalm.[40] Reverse eternal spiral – the word is my heart and is written on my heart, sealed to Self Being.

Morning notes: "High estate individual" (spoken within). "Pete says he likes you" (female voice). Friends above and friends below. To live this, bring all attention to moment of movement and thought – One. Power, enabled, creating every movement, larger and greater movement of Word – actualized. I am feeling, sensing, imagining – manifesting.

Vision and notes: A face up close. Faint lines are visible. Ageless.

---

[40] Opening verse: *The Lord is my shepherd; I shall not want.* There is nothing to want or need; there is no need to strive or attain.

"PERFECT LOVE CASTS OUT FEAR. ONLY PERFECT LOVE EXISTS. IF THERE IS FEAR, IT PRODUCES A STATE THAT DOES NOT EXIST. BELIEVE THIS AND I WILL BE FREE."

Only God established this solution and this faith is His Gift. God established truth. I AM His Establishment. God has faith in me, for I AM Him Self.

All aspects of fear are untrue because they do not exist at the created level and so do not exist at all. To the extent I am willing to submit my beliefs to this test, to that extent are my perceptions corrected.

Oh, God, I hear you calling me to truth. Search me, Lord, for errors to be corrected.

Error: The beliefs of up and down in space, gravity. Time.

Limitations: Eating, digestion. Certain foods are easier, better, best, and not good for digestion. This is a lump of limitation.

Fear: Caution and hesitancy of muscle movement; weak knees, hips, spine, joints, stomach muscles, bladder, core – lack of circulation.

Truth: Digestion – Body is spirit. Created to function perfectly and automatically, like breathing. Established by Creator, One in God. All food is blessed by God for our delight. The earth is the Lord's and the fullness thereof. Greater is He that is in me than he that is in the world.

When we are afraid of anything, we give it power over us. We believe in what we value. Fear is valuing error. This destroys peace. The "peace of God which passes understanding" is totally incapable of being shaken by error. It denies the power of anything not of God to affect one. This brings error to light. Since error and darkness ae the same, it corrects itself automatically. I deny error can hurt me.

My fearful thoughts cannot harm me. There is one power only, and it is love. Error, fear, do not exist. My mind is an extension of God Mind and creates only love, harmony, peace, and joy.

I want a miracle. My intention is to hold only to right mind.[41] I entered deeply into His presence with awareness. I need your Truth spoken to heal me of fear. Speak the Word and I shall be healed. "Let go." I felt myself free falling with no fear. "Take a breath." I felt a deep breath. Resting, at peace.

New depth in Self. I feel Truth within me. Christ gave me *itself* freely given. I am empowered from on high. My mind creates its highest idea. I am great Love gifted of my Father. I give my mind back to God, Self to will and do of It's good pleasure to save the world He created.

Discomfort arises to bring to awareness to the need for correction in the mind. Only the mind is capable of illumination. Spirit is illuminated. Body is brought into alignment with the mind that looks beyond the body to the Light, to Truth of God. We, as children of God, are entitled to the perfect comfort and peace that come from trust. God is perfect trust. *It* Self, my Self is God manifested.

---

[41] Right-minded (-brained): creative, artistic; left-minded (-brained): logical analytical, objective.

Mystical experience: I feel with inner vision. When it is over, I ask for thoughts and words to describe and understand it. This is what I was given: I am aware of lying prone. I am moving forward. Close on my right is a tall, beautiful man pedaling a large wheel in front of him as he sits. He takes my right hand in his left hand and holds it. My hand is closed. He opens it by interlocking his fingers with mine. I feel and see him do it. I say, "I love you." Now I am pedaling while lying prone and I wonder how my right foot does not get caught in the big wheel that is moving so fast. Now I am forced to stop pedaling. I can't move. I felt the force stop me. I am now pumping a bicycle up a steep hill. I feel my lungs breathing deeply and my chest muscles working. Now I am at the top on level ground. I feel the ease of moving and turning. I am at ease. A man on a bicycle rides through this space, also with ease. Three five–year–old children are riding Big Wheel bikes into this space. I feel their energy and excitement at their power and strength. Now I am home in the garage. I wonder whether to buy a girl's or a boy's bike to have. It's more enjoyable to share the journey.

Dream: I am in a restaurant kitchen, in the back. My attention is drawn to a worker in bare feet, a hulky man, walking, and his body maneuvering strangely, not normal. He seems unconscious of himself. I think, " Someday it will come back at you, walking barefoot on concrete." I go out front to the counter to order. Three men are behind the counter. They are all healthy, hardy–looking men. I speak to the one nearest me. "I'll have [breakfast] with two paper plates (picturing them separate). I take that back. Just one." The man wrote my order down and talked to me in a low voice with an accent. I couldn't understand him. He didn't give me a check. He just tore the slip off. I then spoke to the next man, and asked, "How can I pay? I don't know the amount I owe." He didn't answer me; he just looked into my eyes. I notice how much he looks like the other man. I then address the third man. He is higher up and behind the others, as if he were at a cash register. "Are they brothers?" "No, he's his father." They look the same age. "No payment due. I am free."

While reviewing the dream, I realize I am not excused; I am exonerated.[42] Years ago, a friend told me that walking barefoot on concrete, as I always did, causes female problems.

Night in bed with eyes closed: Face of Jesus appeared and a beam of light came to me.

I had been coughing. Thought: Is this pneumonia? I claimed Jesus with me in a place apart, watching and listening, distancing and not identifying with the cough, with Patricia's cough. I asked, "Can we give it comfort?" "It doesn't need it. It's just going through the motions the mind needs to act out. If you but touch it, it will stop." I put my finger to throat. I felt quiet, peace – no cough. I was then a child in bed and Daddy was coughing. I wanted to touch him to comfort him, to hug him. He was shaking. I felt his pain and longed to relieve it.

Dream: Throwing things away. There was a picture of Jesus praying in the garden. "I don't want to get rid of this." It became real – I was part of the picture with Him. Felt he was praying for me. "Why are you always praying?" "I'm not praying words. It's

---

[42] Relieved of a responsibility, obligation, hardship; clear of accusation.

a power, continuous thought in mind, always available. I AM one with this *it*. Call for help and I AM right here."

February 24

Meditation: Lord, I want to trust these muscles to be strong. "Muscles have no life of their own, only the life my Consciousness gives them. I, your Savior, Am mighty and strong. The universe is held in place by my Consciousness, as it has none of its own. It cannot trust or fear. You have claimed your muscles as tender and weak, so they are not strong.

The Word is in your mouth. It is I, the Lord God Almighty, who worketh; not you, Patricia, in mortal body – mind. You are the beholder of all. I am the doer, the cause. Step out on faith in me, the mighty God. Nothing else can be trusted. There is nothing else. Your body is Holy and only Holy Mind lives it – in it and through it. Body is manifestation of Immortal God. Mortal mind does not exist. Only God."

Meditation: I heard and knew an egg cracked open. What is the meaning? *"You have gone on ahead."* "No, no, no – such craziness. Stop. I AM one. I AM the Lord thy God. Thou shalt have no other Gods before me. Thou shalt not take the name of the Lord thy God in vain. Thou shalt not curse, swear, or conscious lie. I cannot lie. I am holy, I am true, I am God of God – there is no other." I saw a mother cow with a calf alongside her. God – Life – Love is only Cause. There is no other. Egg – new life I am empowered within – new growth in consciousness and understanding. Cow – I love cow – warm feeling of being fed warm milk right from cow. Calf causes pain. She stepped on my foot. I screamed – did something wrong. I felt ashamed and my stomach felt fear. I tried to pull my foot out – pain lodged in hip – not strong enough – weak – lie. A belief muscles were not strong enough. I am strong in the Lord and in the power of His might. He in me.

I invited Jesus Christ into that memory. I felt weak. He told me to lie down on a grassy hill. I asked what He could do. He put one hand on my foot, the other on my hip. "My love covers all things. You are a brave little girl." I felt warm and relaxed. I am restored in belief in my soul faith. I am strong. I am not ashamed of my childlike trust. I rest assured.

Meditation: Speak, Lord. I hear and receive. I wait in my deepest heart. "Yes, I live in you. I AM One. I AM Only. I AM. I AM Greater. I AM Love. I AM All!"

Awoke in Reality of Love. Thought *Feels Real* – Thought and Word empowered in expression – Words and Thoughts of who and what I AM in Christ are energy field empowered in light, in Visual Mind's Eye. Thought and Word expressed are connected – One visible, manifested thought. Connected, not separate.

Realization: My soul is restored, means Belief – Faith is restored – conscious understanding of Truth. Before, I believed the words. Now, I understand them. Restored is Spirit of Truth – Faith in Self – One. Faith is Word in Action – Manifested – I AM Faith in Action. I AM Faith Manifesting Spirit – Truth. Thank you.

You have been with me always. You never left me. You speak truth in my thoughts. You are my thoughts. You are my remembrance. You live my Soul – One. I AM Living Soul Forever, and Forever and Forever Living Soul of God. You, I AM.

Remembrance, I AM Memory in Truth. Only Truth IS. I remembered and declared Your Promises. I AM Living Promise.

Meditation: Affirmation – God IS Divine Extravagance Continuously giving ITSELF completely away. To consciously realize this is *knowing*. I AM Divine Magnificence. I AM Living Diving Magnificence. I AM Glory of my Father. The Father IS Glorified in *me*. I AM Divine Exuberance.

Morning note: *I KNOW HE IS CALL TO TRUTH.*

Night notes: "I didn't receive my pay." "What, am I hurting for some reason?" Help, Holy One. You are answer to call for Truth. Help.

"We are the only two there are – You and Me." "I must be hurting something about myself." "Is that clear?" And I'm wondering, is that clear?

"Lord, speak to me that I may speak in living echoes of Thy Word." (I hated pain. I gave it power.) "I am all good. I cannot hurt myself." "There is no place for pain to come from." "I am the Lord thy God. There is no other." "No God of pain." (Pain is not.) (God could not create pain. It does not exist.) "There are not two of us. I AM God of Love and Goodness." "There is no other." (I felt a discomfort in my hips. I asked for help. Everyone who asks, receives.)

And then I had a momentous realization:

How can I hate pain or fear it? There is NO such thing. There is Only a world of Love – One God of All – Love.

Night notes: "You never went all the way."

135

Morning notes: "Can we play?" "Yes, we have play here."
Response came in a childhood song: Playmate, come out and play
with me and bring your dollies three, climb up my apple tree.
Look down my rain barrel, slide down my cellar door, and we'll
be jolly friends forever more.

Early morning: I stood in moonlight, felt and saw light on my
forehead. I rise, I live, I know I AM.

Morning notes: "I withdraw into sanctum plus."

When body gets my attention, I know it is Mind speaking truth,
Life expressing its Holiest, Majestic Self.

I am free to support my Self as I am created to. I am free to hold
myself in a healthy position as I am created to. I am promise
fulfilled. I am answer to call. I am Voice. Oh, such glory bestowed
in Source, my Heavenly Father of All Life. I am Queen of my
Kingdom, Given to share with all. All is a gift to use and enjoy.

Reiki and prayer to Alyssa, 8:30 p.m.: I pictured my hands on her
throat and felt her anxiety and upset stomach. I heard myself say,
"Stop." "What?" "This line of action. It is not what you really
want. I bring peace – love." She received. Thank you, Dear One.
Not to focus on error.

"It amazes me that, with all this, it is still not coming unto me,
what is this world?" I *should* be getting this. I *can't believe* that,
with all that has been revealed from subconscious. I *won't* believe.
How can it *not* come unto me? How can it not reveal itself to me?
What is this world?

"THIS WORLD IS AN ORGASM – A CONTINUOUS SPIRITUAL ORGASM – COMMUNION (INTERCOURSING) OF SUBCONSCIOUS, MIND, AND SPIRIT." I had never asked.

More messages arise from subconscious.[43]

I can't do anything without getting hurt, without hurting myself. No matter which way you turn, it's always one thing or another. It's always something. No! The messages now changed to the positive from conscious mind. There is always something to cling to – truth. Truth is always. Truth is all there is.

I AM comforter. I AM up, down, in, out, sideways, either way. You can't move out of me. I can't move out of my Self.

Meditation: "Let's go play, Patsy Ann."[44] Aware of limiting thoughts from subconscious: Life is not always easy. Corrected: Life is always easy.

Can't keep your stuff straight. Corrected: I am responsible only to keep my stuff straight, to keep my thoughts (movement) in line with Spirit.

Night notes: "You ask for the word; I have given you the word. Issue it forth from your mouth, O man. To you who do not read the signs, no more shall be given. The word is hidden in your heart. Trust in the Lord."

Nighttime: My hips are screaming. Help, comforter. I sleep and am awakened to "I beat him." Four–year–old Doug pulled down his shorts and shook his penis at a friend, laughing as he did so.

---

[43] To the clear light of conscious mind, the Truth which transforms them.

[44] Another name for Patricia as a child.

He thought it was funny. I spanked him so hard I had a bruise on my palm. Fear arose inside me. I cannot allow this. As a child, Patsy Ann stayed with a neighbor family while Mommy and Daddy worked. The neighbor's son was a tease. One day, while Patsy Ann was sitting on the outhouse seat, the boy quietly lifted the back drop and with a long stick touched her fanny. She was really upset and crying when the boy's older sister asked her what was wrong. When Patsy Ann explained, the sister told her father, who gave her brother a beating. I was responsible for another's pain. Fear of peeing.

Now I fear sitting. I fear the pain I feel as my torso settles into my hips. It feels sharp and shocking, like the experience in the outhouse. Twenty–five years ago, I confessed to my son, with great remorse, the unjustified beating he had received. I also explained that it was my "stuff" coming up.

The last part of my body to hold out were my arms, which were held by a tight, hard muscle up my spine. I listened carefully to what my arms had to tell me: move and lift a small object with one hand at a time. Left arm (subconscious) held to not hurting anyone, including me. Be gentle to self. As I gave attention to that arm and heard its message, my arms became free.

I realized I had developed a hands-off mentality, to stay out of things.

I went to the Bible to turn my mind to truth. As I went back to bed, I said, "Turn it over to God. It's too much to take in right now." No! I must consciously understand Truth – See Truth – Know Truth. I do, and I AM free.

The Old Testament: What we as man believe and fear, we testify to and prove it true.

The New Testament: Jesus Christ is Truth revealed, All good, One God.

Matthew 6:3: Let not your left hand (your subconscious) know what your right hand is doing (thinking, acting).[45]

I am in bed on my back, a cough awakens me. Something comes into my throat. I want it out. Sexual abuse, semen, pee, a distinct odor is about me. It is in me!

The night was uncomfortable. I was lying on my back and felt the urge to move. My legs wanted to kick but held back in fear of hurting myself. I turned on my side and was aware of the bottom leg feeling numb, the foot resting on it felt like a great pressure weighing one hundred pounds.

Felt a pain in the left kidney area where the muscle is tight. Also felt tenderness in upper right arm when pressed.

Meditation: Kidneys are purifiers. I AM pure. The kidneys are in the right place, the fit place as their function. Pure blood – clean intent and purpose of mind. What obstructs its flow is transformed to pure understanding of Self. I allowed my feet to kick at a child's level of strength while letting my arms and hands "beat off" the weight of responsibility for the pain or hurt of another. In awareness of Holy Truth, I kicked and beat "life" into these bones, enlivening them.

---

[45] But when you give to the needy, do not let your left hand know what your right hand is doing (English Standard Version of the Bible).

Them bones, them bones, them Life bones.

Morning notes: "And you get it over with [pain]." I never will. I am the experience – It. "A fence is a line – if you put it in the picture, you must designate[46] if you are before or after." I saw a white fence standing vertical to green grass, dividing it. "I knew she'd find it" and "Two lines, both sides [of the fence]."

I was numb in my toes and the side of my left leg. "I don't have sides." "I AM all sides." "*It* is not valuable." "IT is." "IT is not." IT is and...

Meaning of the word *illusion*: A false perception or conception of where one is or what one sees – false – pain is false – an unreal or misleading appearance or image. Attention to my lower right jaw. "God is here." "Go ahead, do launching.[47]" Are you kidding?

"I am going within." "A hotel key opens the door." "I am the light that shines forever." "I bring understanding to the darkened place." "I'm getting the soap." "Talking in Japanese is so intelligent." Symbol: Feeling responsible for Mother's pain that is stored in my memory as guilt, and it relates to the numbness in my legs. The numbness keeps my legs from moving over the fence or block (guilt) to the other side. While practicing generational healing in Gestalt Pastoral Care, it was revealed to me in a vision of a past lifetime that my dad and I were Japanese. He was the

---

[46] *Designate*: point out, indicate, specify, name, entitle; name for an office or duty; appoint to indicate and set apart for a specific purpose, office, or duty; chosen, but not yet installed (Webster's Dictionary).

[47] *Launch*: Hurl, discharge, send off (as a weapon or a verbal attack); cause a newly built vessel to slide from land into water, set afloat, set in operation; launch out of space and out of time.

offended young boy and I was the offender. A learning is revealed to provide understanding and healing, and for taking conscious responsibility for our part in the evolving of Consciousness, God, Infinite Mind – expanding Self.

Meditation: 3-hour session: Felt deep gratitude to God and to all who draw me to him – every friend, author, Bible figure, and those who came to me. All blessed me.

Image of a man speaking to me: "Listen." "I am open to understanding." "I am understanding." "I am under – standing." "I am basic platform." "I am form." "I am all."

Night image: Two undefined spirit bodies dancing as one. They separate and fuse as one. They separate again – always touching. One.

Night image: View of a bicycle frame where it joins for the pedals. There were no pedals. The frame was fused together. Fusion.

Awoke with urge to stretch my legs. Fear of pain. Conflict – inner urge to move – I resist in fear of pain.

I am an opening flower – soft, tender, living into ever new tenderness – sensitivity. I feel I am a bother to Ed. Part of me, an old habit wants to do. Old belief that I am a bother, a pain. I feel uncomfortable being a bother. I am holy spirit. I am love and life to all I encounter.

I heard within me the sound of twelve drops in my left ear, twelfth chakra open to finer and higher vibration. What does this mean? I am receiving more light and help from higher mind.

Conflict: Urge to stretch and move – hold back – resist in fear of pain – seems to be an automatic body response. Don't stretch or move, like the movement of pushing to birth a child feels like a bowel movement and I want to hold back. Pain brings immediate resistance and tightening of my body because my subconscious holds the belief that pain is bad and leads to death. I have believed the body is intelligent and speaks to me. I depend on it to reveal errors in others to be corrected. I am now aware and conscious of greater sensitivity, sexuality has been restored with greater intuition. I choose to live in this sensitive, delicate place, and an old habit part of me wants to do automatically. I am not fully awakened. Conflict. What am I not understanding? I want resolve.

Donna said, "Remember practicing the presence of God. I am one with whatever I am doing, as God is doing it through me. Walking in baby steps. Back up and learn from the past by watching others act mindlessly." Yoga walk in awareness. Once we experience truth, we can never choose the old way. I receive Reiki to address my conflict. Pain or discomfort slows my physical movement down while inner healing of my muscles takes place. All is in perfect order. I am center of the universe. I am always in perfect alignment and place. I am fitted together by Mind of Christ.

Night image: A pine tree was falling toward me. My world was about to crash. "He was talking to the phony party." "Hurry up, phony party. Just tell me about it." (This voice was harsh and crude. At the time I did not know this was a premonition of Ed leaving. I was in denial about Ed dying).

I received Reiki from a friend. She felt the slow, deliberate walk of an elephant. They eat what other animals refuse. I digest all thoughts: I process all thoughts as profitable and life sustaining. I walk deliberately empowered to my goal of function and purpose – everlasting One life of body, mind, and spirit – inseparable.

MY WALK LEAVES MY IMPRINT IN THE SANDS OF TIME – AWARENESS OF TRUTH – ONE GOD.

There is no need to fear making a wrong choice. There is only good to choose, once we name it so.

I am feeling more comfortable sitting at the right hand of God.

Meditation: 4-hour session on my back: I am relaxed, quiet – all life, all love of the universe is mine. Image: Open right hand in front of me. I smelled lily of the valley and hay. I felt the massive body of elephant and his gentle power in his legs. Faces of people who came to help.

Images: An eye with two rays shooting from it; an eye with three rays shooting from it; an eye with four rays shooting from it; an eye with five rays shooting from it; and a crystal shape in the form of a six–petal flower of life.

After each experience, I was aware of breathing fast and light. I am center of the universe. What do I want? I waited for words to be given. To move as one body, mind, and spirit – freely. This means I trust and have faith in God in my Christ Mind, my Self. When images of faces appeared, I felt pressure in my sacroiliac joint, but not pain. It had been holding fear and resistance. I arose from a reclined position very slowly, in awareness of my movement, and breathing into each movement. My arms were more relaxed. I was to remain in place while correction was made through Spirit at the center of Self.

Meditation: I am growing in faith as a living, moving being in Christ Mind, Breath of life, awareness.

Realization: This physical posture and condition looks, acts, and feels like Jack Smith, a friend of Mother's. I was jealous of him and the attention she gave him when I was a child. I *hated* him. I never got enough of her attention. I now feel the pain and need Jack lived with. His spine had been crushed. I understand that his friendship with my mother filled his need for love and happiness. I forgive myself. I am willing to have cause and truth revealed.

Reiki with Esther: She sees a beech tree across the street. Spine, the tree of life. There is an evergreen tree. Its needles are nerves from the spine that feed the trunk of the body. "For the joy set before him, he endured the cross" (the tree). Jack's spine had been broken in a previous life and he lost his life. A horse was responsible. Esther saw pictures of my muscles outlined, muscles that were holding in guilt and shame. The pelvic girdle and psoas muscles are not to hold back life, to prevent birth; instead, they are to move it out into life. The discs and vertebra were seen with a bright light running down my spine like lightning, that was the horse's mane. Muscle is a living stream of life. Truth had to be told. I affirmed my muscles and spine with gratefulness. They were held in a frozen (unmovable, unmoving) condition and supported me. Now muscles are holding until all of abdomen (core) is in place. This is Grace.

144

January 7, 2014

Today, my beloved, you went Home.

You fulfilled the council of your heart to be the best husband, father, and grandfather you could possibly be.

Always true to us, your family, and yourself: a real man.

All our love is with you on your heavenly journey, as yours is forever with us.

"So take the sweetest phrases the world has ever known and make believe I said them all to you." Tony Bennett sang these words in the Bing Crosby song "I Can't Begin to Tell You." It was the last show Ed and I attended at the Hershey Theater.

Meditation: *A MYSTICAL EXPERIENCE. COMMUNION BREAD WAS PUT IN MY MOUTH. A HAND CORRECTED MY KNEE.*

Upon waking in the morning: I went to sleep on my back and woke on my side. I felt my body stretch within – quivery. No fear. I am trusting my Self, my Soul.

Night notes: "Your journey is over."

After waking, I heard a groan that was like Ed's groan before he died. "Woman." It was an urgent call. "The more you see, the more your eyes behold reality."

Night notes: I am sitting on Ed's lap looking into his left eye. I am looking at you eye to eye, soul to soul. His eye was not the same as his physical eye had been. I see him differently. I looked at my grandson John, eye to eye, and saw him the same.

"I am a witness." This is her graduation day. Here everything has been going on. And how are you doing? Full of hope and expectancy of a new day?" Yes, I respond. "Enjoy my love. You are my love."

I am sitting on a toilet. A friend comes in and says, "Do you mind?" "Not at all. We're all the same. Different smells, maybe." I saw a large, glowing light. Opened my eyes and saw the light on the ceiling. I am expanded light, Consciousness today. I am Light of Light, mind. I touched my Savior and realized the kingdom of

Heaven I sought. I am One with all Life, God. Felt a vibration gradually fill me: hands, feet, and head, then down my spine through my hips. I was consciously aware of Spirit's presence – witness to it. I am vibration, energy, Holy Spirit, Life – my birthright. Set this wondrous spirit free. Spirit of the living God, light afresh on me – light – word – vibration – every second – continuously. When the Lord sets you free, you are free in deed, in doing.

After a counseling session with Doris Stoltzfus[48], I realized changing position is painful. I don't have to leave home now, my life with Ed. Don't have to think about it now. I can't imagine life alone, "out there." I would like to enjoy life. My incentive is to be well. I'm avoiding change, holding onto the past; I don't want to move. It takes a lot of energy to keep myself in the same position, resisting change – fear of movement – tension – holding back. Awareness of life as I have experienced it on earth is over. I have had a beautiful and full life and I anticipate an even more beautiful and greater life as I live in deeper awareness of the Kingdom within me. I am receiver of countless gifts and I am animated with these gifts as I share them. It is your way I follow, Lord, to the fulfillment of your purpose for me. You are the desire of my heart. My life on earth is far from over. The best is yet to come. Yahoo!

I am the daughter of the King of Righteousness. I am born of Eternal Righteousness, Infinite Life, Power, Love, and Peace. I am Eternal Spirit, expressing and manifesting as individual Spirit Body. I am Love. I love You. My body with all my heart vibrates

---

[48] Thomas's mother-in-law.

harmony in You. Choose this vibration of Love, which you are, for I give you my Love and I am Life. I am righteous position always. My body is Spirit – not filled with – it *is* Living Spirit. My body is deemed Holy. It cannot be left behind. Its comfort had been out of place. In God we trust. This is sacred trust – sealed in truth in Christ.

Meditation: I saw a fighter boxing shadows, illusions. This is making me strong. Error. I am all strength. I have a fear of hearing commercials. If I think this, it will happen. I fear my mind will create other than good. Impossible. Good is the only power. Body is glorious. Life and time are a gift to declare this glory. Only in time can we learn this.

"I am with you. Write a new story on backs.[49] I AM author."

The living word communes in me. I AM Word: feeling, hearing, experience. *I know truth* intimately in my body. I know my body as sacred, holy, complete; my spirit communes with itself within my sacred body, the body of Christ – living word of the Father. I abide in Christ and Christ in me. This is the law. Mind instructs me at night, makes known to me the path of life, shines light and intelligence. I ask, and am answered. *I MUST ASK.*

Muscle spasms. My sister, Jane, is visiting me. We prayed and she read the Bible to me and slept in my room.

I called my grandson John to come on Sunday when Jane leaves. I am afraid to be alone. I feel sympathy for others who suffer fear. I need to wake up to their true identity and my own, and bring

---

[49] Physical back or past events.

them to my level of spirit, love them beyond humanness. All I am is of God. No human element enters this relationship. All I possess in Consciousness is mine – it is my recognition of an invisible spiritual tie binding me in an eternal brotherhood of love. Body is perfect, immortal and eternal as soul, God, the principle of body.

Vision: Two men are standing close together. A scene behind them moved to the left. They were motionless.

"Where is your father?" I asked Jesus. "I know I go straight to the Father." I feel more deeply my identity as a Son of God. I wept and wept for two hours, communing with my Father. I waited on Him and felt received in His presence. I looked right up close into a dog's eye. I was bowed on the floor. A great light shone in its eye. I am always in His eye. His eye is ever on me. I am drawn to God through the Son. Not only me, Lord, but all you have brought to me. I crowded them before me. Today I realize I do nothing except open Self to receive.

I awoke with an understanding: *THE SON WAS IN THE FATHER BEFORE THE WORLD WAS CREATED. I HAVE ALWAYS BEEN, AND ETERNALLY SHALL BE, IN THE FATHER. I CANNOT BE MOVED.* God so loved the world that He gave His only begotten Son, that whosoever believed in the Son, begotten of God, has eternal life. *HOW DEEPLY SECURE AND BELOVED OF GOD I AM.*

I listen for the Word to come to my thought and live in my heart. This Word already lives in my heart and continually comes to my thought. This Word *is* my thought. This Word lives, my heart. I *feel* this Word vibrating within this house of God.

I conceive this life. I express this life. I AM this life. *Glory, Glory, Glory. Love, Love, Love. Beauty, Beauty, Beauty.* I AM harmony expressing beauty. All I AM, I share with All Life. I AM ALL Goodness. I AM ALL Power. I AM a Gentle, Strong, Faith-full Being. This Word lives me. I live this Word. I trust SELF. I AM ALL Life. I AM ALL Energy. I AM ALL. There are no mistakes, no errors. I AM every thought. I AM every act, every movement. Feeling weakness is my strength.

I AM LOVE. I overcome all. I AM the only way. Glory, Glory, Glory. Tears of joy. A glorious light is within me – gold, green, lavender, and pink, shining in and through this House of God. This Light of Lights, true God of true God. Begotten, not made. Today, Light shines clearly, directly from the heart of God.

Morning thoughts: *God Wills me Well. All Life Wills me Well. All Life is of God. Life blesses me with all blessings. All Life is within me. I AM in all Life. Space is Life. Live into the spaces.*

Pain in my stomach – felt tight. Was it the oranges? Too much acid? Not enough? A belief in error. We are to have power over our minds and bodies. Our minds are our servants. Change my mind. "Love allows all things." Holy One, I give you full sway over my thoughts. "There is only love – no bad, or better – there is only good." All things are good for us. Our Father in Heaven declares it so. Seal truth to my heart. Thank you for revealing error.

150

My heart opened to the beautiful, tender love I felt for my grandson, John, as a baby and child. That love is me. I am open to feeling this tender heart with awareness in Christ Mind Consciousness of Self. Love created me. Love begot me. Love is the attention I desire and give my Self.

On the porch, my friends, the trees, were speaking. They reach out with their branches, embracing me through their leaves breathing a perfume of Love; of Love living ITSELF from the womb of Being. Ah, the gentle surrender of all form to the heart of Love.

Night notes: Donna is so sensitive. She is about to have a million-dollar baby; a picture scrolled quickly past my view. I am full moon. Under me is all light, no darkness.

Night image: A large snake is lying around the foot of our large tulip tree. Kundalini energy at the base of spine.

Meditation: Saw Flower of Life on my back.

Meditation: Angel appeared.

Meditation: Saw a page of music.

Felt tenderly drawn into great compassion for all who suffer. Tears ran freely. I sat up sobbing and moaning for all in pain, that they open to receive the great gifts of the Holy One I acknowledge within, bringing peace and joy. My prayer was received and answered as tears and wailing became joyful and exuberant, causing my spirit to dance within me. All is well. Enjoy.

Morning note: "Not by might nor by power, but by my spirit saith the Lord of Awareness – goodness of Spiritual Being." I asked John, Donna, and Esther to support me in prayer for this.

Meditation: I AM open to greater awareness of realization of my complete oneness with spirit. I felt pressure on my left ear. Speak, Lord, thy servant heareth. "Go into silence." "I AM here, hear?" I felt pressure in my bottom to move my bowels. Sitting on the toilet, I said, "I wait on the Lord," (the Holy Spirit is movement), meaning that I will wait for this. "The Lord is a very present help in trouble." I don't need to wait. The Holy Spirit always answers immediately. I realized I believed I was waiting for One outside of me to come. Jesus Christ told the disciples to wait until He sent the comforter. Now I AM raised with Christ to the Heavenly places. I AM seated at the right hand of God. I AM the right hand of God. God has already given me all goodness and spirit in the son which I AM in Christ. I AM the Lord I AM waiting on, not for. Realization of being all I AM in Spirit and Body – One in substance. These truths are the law to my own being as I realize them.

LIVE IN ANTICIPATION – EXPECTANCY OF RECEIVING ALL GOOD. YES.

"There is no such thing as tension, only God, Life, movement." I see the image of a moon globe head on shoulders. It's a view of my back. A left hand is on my left shoulder. Subconscious is glowing and clear.

Image: A bowl and a hand with a spoon skillfully and gracefully removing the contents. A vessel of clay pottery being cleansed. "A parcel is being delivered." Ohhhhrum – high vibration – frequency – Kingdom of Heaven. The vessel is cleansed. I can now receive consciously, claiming the Kingdom within. Fear is gone. Fresh understanding of body language from a new point of clarity. Need to support right hand movement by employing left hand. Right hand is weak of itself. The other half is no longer automatically supporting it. I am an individual finding a way to operate, live life on my own, and move into it.

Changing positions: I ease myself into life gently and surely, feeling my way as I go. What "feels" life giving? Walking, with my abdomen extended as I carry a heavy load while resisting energy movement and flow of life. I now choose to let it free – consciously in mind. No longer leaning back on the past. I will do this.

Tom reminded me that everyone has a fear of being alone since the illusion of separation from God.

Night notes: If anything needs to be brought to my awareness, it will be. Word *unhappy*. I saw Ed and Tom unhappy. This is error; false self. See others only as son of God, perfect, peace, joy, and love.

I AM THE CHRIST, THE VERY PRESENCE OF GOD, LIVING FROM THE STANDPOINT OF LETTING INFINITY POUR THROUGH ME.

I AM HEIR OF GOD, JOINT HEIR WITH CHRIST, THEREFORE, I AM THAT PLACE THROUGH WHICH GOD IS POURING. CHRIST THE SPIRIT OF GOD LIVING AS ME, DOES ALL THINGS.

The Lord exercises loving kindness, judgment, and righteousness in the earth. I'm not "feeling" happy in the Kingdom of Heaven.

Meditation prayer with John: The kingdom has been given to me. I consciously received it. I make a choice to live in it moment by moment. I simply choose my identity. I am Spirit. All I see is spirit being manifested as everyone and everything. I choose to "feel" presence of Life, the exuberance in me and all. I feel happy. I always feel good around Donna. She is happy and it extends from her.

Happy feeling did not last. What's wrong with me?

Night notes: I feel I am being held a prisoner. Of what? I felt a craziness in a small corner of my mind. Picture of myself feeling crazy and acting out of control. I feel severed from the whole – cut off.

Meditation: I realized I am saved WHOLE, not apart from. There is no part of eternity. The door is unlocked. I am free to walk, to move freely and easily. Be gentle with this body; it has been locked in place for a long time. It responds to gentle spirit care. I can't lose bladder or uterus, no part can be lost, for there is not part out of whole. These muscles are also tender and need spiritual support. God is all present in abdomen. Feel His presence. All is perfect order, place, and harmony.

Meditation: I am living breath of all wisdom, presence, and power. I animate this body of wisdom and power through, and in, my presence. I am changeless and ageless.

Word of God, Christ transforms – transfigures. Super Natural Bread of Heaven.

Muscles felt tired. I gave heartfelt thanks for life, movement, and freedom I have gained. Felt a deep gratitude for nature, creation, family, friends, and my Holy Spirit. The Lord tends to me; my every need is provided. I saw him pouring oil on the wound in my hip and oil on my head, healing my mind from the belief I was severed from Him. I am saved from destruction, thanks be to God. I am already healed, whole. Enlighten me to this truth. He said, "There is no wound to heal." There never was, or could be, a separation. I feel I have come full circle.

Meditation: God does not stop or start, is not here or there, is not this side or that side, not top or bottom, inside or outside. God IS unending, all powerful, life. This life I am is God expressing in me, manifesting His Allness, Presence, Power, Light, Love.

Night notes: "All power is given to me in Heaven and Earth." "I gave this to her." A little girl handing me a gift.

Night notes: "Great is thy Faithfulness." I heard the sound of the note C, an octave above middle C, played on the piano.

Sympathy notes were pain – their pain, not mine. I did not FEEL anything.

Image: I saw a clean, white page turning. "I'm turning a new page." Awoke and sat up immediately for the first time. I feel fresh – new day.

A MYSTICAL EXPERIENCE. JESUS CHRIST CAME AND PUT HIS HANDS ON BOTH SIDES OF MY HEAD. I FELT THE TOUCH. THEN HE KISSED THE TOP OF MY HEAD. I SAW A THRONE WITH AN INDISTINCT FIGURE ON IT AND THE FACE WAS JESUS. I GAVE HIM MY MIND TO HOLD. (Meditation)

Upon waking: "I am the structure of this Being." "What is your name, Patricia?" "Patricia Roedema." "Find the missing link." "There can't be a missing link." I then felt a tremendous enlarging and expanding occur in my mind. "Feeling." Words of a song came to mind – the first since Ed passed.

Night notes: I AM living into unknown with awareness. We think we know tomorrow by yesterday. We live in the past. I feel this understanding *NOW – NOW* as I move into new space. Space felt by Ed's absence. Space available as this body functions and moves into it.

I – I – I – live into this space as feeling led by thinking.

The past feels heavy, like a shroud over me preventing life's emergence. Life wins over, popping up like new green leaves standing forth from empty space where they previously were not.

Life draws me forth and claims its own. I cannot hold it back. Yet, resistance is felt.

What is this feeling unlike all life? I AM New Form, New Birth. I am expression of Life *NOW – NOW*.

What am I *NOW*? Who am I? What am I? I am tiny speck in unknown, unnamed, space.

I hear heart. I recognize and feel heart. I AM heart. I feel into Self and expand and flow into all movement. I AM heart, Life, movement. I AM sound – movement, speaking. I do not hear my expanded movement as blood moving through this body.

A speck of what? A speck is separate. I AM life, movement, sound, energy – one with all Heart, Life, Movement, Energy.

A thought enters and then another: I AM endless thought. Am I a speck until I feel I am endless? Until I feel one with all?

Night notes: Now, my God, One with my Lord, I turn to you. Praise, Honor, and Blessing to the King of Kings, Now and forevermore. Grace comes through Jesus Christ who gives us the victory. I rest in You. Amen and Amen.

Donna and I sat in silence for an hour. I felt her gift to me. What a treasure she is. She is of myself. In human terms, bodies are a glimmer of what I am to my God, my Self, my Messiah.

In bed: My leg was twitchy and would not be still. "I am life moving in and through you, my Self. You have been still long enough. I am energy moving you. Allow me." All movements from side to side are relaxing the tight muscles, gently exercising them.

Meditation: I am son of God. I am sustained in and by the heart of Love in harmony with all good and Life. I am Newborn today to greater goodness to express through me. This is the Eternal Way of Life. I am this unfolding. I am God, complete manifestation. I am One Patricia. I have brought you here. Every step of the way is forever my step, the only Life, Love, and Heart. There is no other. I am Doctor. I touched you in Wisdom, body, and Spirit, One. I am manifesting greater awareness of Self as You. I am You. You are me. I am One, not we. I am new now, forever and ever and ever, greater awareness unfolding. I am all that touches me. I am Life flowing in and through me. I am Mind understanding Self in manifestation. I am in the Father and the Father is in me. We act as one. A new day.

2:00 a.m.: I am standing in the moonlight on the front porch with Max (Tom's dog). Took moon in – claiming it as mine. It lights me through and through, back and front – all light in me. I claim and share it, extending it to all our family group. There is no night, no darkness ever. We all walk in light.

Night notes, 4:00 a.m.: "I Am the One who knows that I Am the One." "One thing, I heard a man get started because of you." "I was trying very hard to stay out of him." Doug.

Meditation, 9:00 a.m.: Chakras. I claim all I AM. I dip deeply into substance. I AM light, all light, all good. I extend to all with warmth and compassion. Felt the root chakra receiving. I included family.

Image: Black and white vertical grid, or a fine veil – understanding – I am reclaiming body by renewal of mind, Life Principle, One.

White light, a pure heart, Christ Mind. I AM Pure Christ Mind, created from heart of Mother God, blue solar plexus (third chakra). I dip deeply into substance of my being, Self. I AM heart of God's heart. Mary brought me to awareness of what I AM and always have been. I AM inherited and established through my creation in Life ITSELF. I AM All with the Father and Holy Spirit. I AM always Center in my universe, forever creating more and more good eternally, fuller, opulence, overflowing to all life.

Green light, thyroid (throat chakra): I AM WORD IN MIND OF GOD. I AM HIS; HE IS MINE. ONE.

Violet light, pineal (sixth chakra): Centered, peaceful, poised, still. Totally aware.

Woman comes with flowers, smiling: "That's all." I mentally acknowledge her. I was not tempted to move out of my place into feelings. The face of Little Flower (Saint) appeared, along with the colors green and violet – an open eye – large, soft, gentle. I opened my eyes and saw an endless yellow Flower of Life pattern on the ceiling. I blinked and it was still there.

"I love you." I appreciate your love for me.

Before sleep: I am in a garden with outstanding orange flowers along the left side and bright yellow flowers alongside them to the right. Chakras are in full bloom.

Gestalt session with Rhoda Glick: I am in judgment and need compassion. I feel warmth in my torso; Jesus is befriending me. We are not separate. He is one with me. "You can do nothing without me, precious child." I feel grateful and guarded against temptation by Truth. I do nothing. There is no judgment without

Jesus. His is righteous. "I love you." This is a day of love. I AM love.

Barbara Gascho's visit: She gave me Reiki. This is our spiritual honeymoon, a spiritual bonding of my deep gratitude for Ed's care of home and me. I've been cared for and always will be by that love. Ed's love and caring is within me. I honor him and myself – our union – by guarding our precious honeymoon on a higher plane and frequency. My gratitude is a sweet, sweet sound to the Ear of life.

Gestalt session with Rhoda: I make all things new. Doug's relationship with his dad is now one of trust.[50] His dad hears him and will help him. Doug will do fantastic artwork, his best. Doug is free of shame of not being the man his dad expected him to be. Ed has no judgment now. (Ed is clear, so Doug feels clear.) Father and son are free in love.

Meditation: Long, deep waves of emotion come to me. A very large flame is burning within me. "Smile" sang in my mind; it was the second song to break forth from within. Thank you, Tony Bennett. Tony sang "Smile" at the last performance Ed and I enjoyed at the Hershey Theater.

Night notes: "I am honest with you. Ten minutes after it is said, I put the power in it." Focusing seventeen seconds yields 2,000 minutes of power to live – life power.[51] This answers my question regarding instant truth and healing. My soul has been restored

---

[50] Doug's dad knew his son was a gifted artist but not using his gifts.

[51] Theory put forth by Esther and Jerry Hicks.

160

and the body follows. All effort put forth is multiplied by thousands in spirit.

"I AM TRUTH, I AM LIFE, I AM HOLY ETERNAL LIVING LIFE."

Dream: A figure with a soft, feminine face and short hair. "I need to go up higher. Is there an elevator? I have a baby. Will you answer me?" Yes. I felt a desire to crawl up in a fetal position and be held. Mentally, I did that. I cried with John.

"Listen to no one. Doubt not your Self. Your path is yours alone. Walk in it. This path is your call home. Nothing can threaten or delay this walk. Your steps are measured by the Infinite Cause of your Being. I give you my word. It is hidden in your heart, my heart. Let not your heart be troubled. Believe in God. Believe also in me, your Holy Spirit Self.

"I am taking you higher in understanding. I have plans for you: a life full of glory in which you fulfill your purpose as my beautiful daughter. You need only give me all your fears, doubts, and questions of yesterday and step into this wonderful life now. Born today. I care for all your needs. All you cannot do for yourself I do and perform in and through you. Behold the goodness of God your perfect Father in Heaven, come to earth as Christ, the Holy Spirit. Where are your fears now? They are not.

"God is sure. God is faithful. God is within. God is without. God *IS*. Breathe in truth with every breath. Feel this Holy Breath flowing through your Consciousness – a living water, a stream you are carried in, cleansing your mind, washing all concerning you, my precious child. I have never left you. Feel my Presence. Feel my Life. Feel my Power. Feel my Love."

Ear is blocked. I hear no one. I only hear and see God's love in all and reflect that back to them.

Reiki from Esther: Be ye perfect as your Father in Heaven is perfect. Illumine me of this truth. Bless you, Friend, through this love you share with me, an understanding of Miriam and Moses.[52] Esther saw a semicircle of swinging plates above me: copper, brass, gold. They were two–thirds the size of a door and represent my future sliding into place. One would slide into place, moving gently. Intricate patterns of lines shaped like vines within each plate. One plate represents life with Ed. Esther felt teary at the tenderness of this life. Each plate represents other people and times in my life. One is half blank with no pattern; it represents our *A Course in Miracles* book group. Plates also tell of unity with all. Continue to be with the spirits of animals passing through vision in my window. One or more has much to teach me. Open Self to John. Interchange between us is meant to benefit each of us greatly. Continue to find ways to laugh together and enjoy.

Reiki from Esther: There was a manila folder with a beautiful clasp on the spine center (the center of the folder). The clasp has beautiful, intricate patterns as do the plates. Open it! It holds a world of possibilities. Message to Esther: Remember to weigh things in the balance.

---

[52] Esther and Patricia found meaning in the relationship of Miriam and Moses, referring to their own friendship.

I open the manila folder. Holy One, reveal the meaning of the contents – words? ideas? picture? – we have prepared through the beautiful life Ed and I lived together. The clasp is a closure. The intricate patterns were woven by our spirits, of our spirits within and of the Great Universal Spirit. I touch this clasp and feel the power of *all life* expressing in me and emanating like fire through my being to All Life. As I touch, I receive and am empowered to give back a thousandfold more. I open the clasp by touching it. The clasp is life. What will I put my hand to today? Touch.

John and I. I am feeling weak and scared; I have no faith. Did I ever have faith? Where is it now? How could I be so strong and sure then and have no strength in faith now? I can't get it of myself. It is a gift. I did nothing to receive it except confess my fear and lack. I throw myself on God's mercy, confessing my emptiness, fear, weakness, wretchedness, and doubt. I resisted sharing with John, but I broke down. He is blessed by this, of course. He opens his heart to hear my truth, from my heart. This is the only gift I can give him, and it is enough. Right now, it is all I am.[53] I remember the words I received yesterday. Where are they now? "I will never leave you. We will walk through this step by step. I will be with you. I have plans for you for a wonderful life." That was yesterday and this is tomorrow. He spoke a promise. Yes, He is with me as I give Him my fears and weakness. He gave me John to be with me. I shed tears of gratitude, wisdom, and understanding. Peace returns. He gave His promise. It is sure.

---

[53] Widow's mite.

Good morning, Holy One. Spring will come to my body and soul. It rests within this very moment. I stop and check in and, yes, it is here. A glow of light appears beneath the still. I go to it.

I feel pain, fear, doubt; am I dying? Donna said, "Don't think that." She is so happy and trusting. I felt that joy and trust. I know that feeling. Remember, anticipation is the most important idea to hold to.

My ear wax is melting. Holy One is corrector. Until now, I saw that as a physical correction. Now I understand. I choose who to relate to, the physical child of fear who did not understand the truth of spirit. I never die. I choose to think life, love, and faith in only God and the power He vested in me. I can sing. I can smile. I can rest in the power of Love. I can choose to feel trusting and empowered. God within me corrected that error. God within my Holy Body corrects in proper order all not in line with His perfect Will, which I am.

Reiki from Donna: Jesus and Mary appeared to me in physical form. I asked for the gift of love and God answered. Jesus Christ and Mary live physically in my body. I realize this truth of love. My body is love, life eternal. Love has come. All fear has gone. I face today as the body of Christ – Love.

Awoke and asked to have a sweet mouth and breath. A young girl came and kissed me on the lips. She came into me through the mouth, bringing me sweet breath.

Esther sent Reiki: (In life, Patricia is suffering from a herniated disc.) First, I saw you were falling about five feet. I see a rock. Next I see possibly a past life. You were with a man and knocked unconscious. It was over a woman, and was extremely traumatic for you. There was a knife – no gun. (However, later on in the revealing of this I sensed that this man gave you a blow with a big stick which led you to fall on the point of a rock. I understood the spot where you fell to be the spot of the present–time herniated disc.) I then saw you hastily packing up and leaving that place. While you were packing up, I saw a leather bag with leather strings that were used to tie it shut.

I see your spirit rising. In the spirit, I understand that I am supposed to open myself to joining you. I see a unicorn, or very spirited horse, riding very fast, full of life and energy. There's no impediment to how fast we go. There's lots of joy, exuberance, abundance, and exhilaration. We're enjoying just the ride, the feeling of it, those hooves and the snorting! (Correction: The snorting was earlier when the two horses met. I now understand that we were two riders doing this.) We're ascending up through different levels, going up through wispy, fog-like, vertical curtains. There are silver and gold threads through them. Each curtain is now a vertical rainbow. We still hear galloping. The curtains are now moving away, rising. I saw a quick picture of a woman of long ago. Her hair was piled up on her head and her dress has a high–necked collar. It's getting warmer (in my room?) and I feel like time and space are compressing. I cannot describe the feeling somehow.

Awoke: A new day. Aware I am out of shock.

Awoke from sleep: Experience in the kitchen: I'm on the side of the desk near the phone. Ed appeared in front of the desk near me. I felt vibrations, as when in communion with Holy Spirit. I did not say "Ed," but sound came forth in uttered vibrations. I feel gratefulness to our Father God, what pleases Him through me – a gift. "Just let me live my life. Let it be pleasing, Lord, to thee." Another song breaks forth.

I am conscious of a deeper power within me that flows forth as a gentle, kindly sympathy, a true brotherliness of loving help to all I contact, inspiring them to higher principle and fullness of life. I am connected to the highest realms of thought – mind. I feel the warmth and thrill of God's tender love as it fills and surrounds me, preparing my way. I love to listen to and obey God's voice. God is responsible for all I am and do.

Rhoda came and gave me communion and prayed: By His stripes we are healed. I don't need to suffer. Breathe in life.

Father in Heaven, for Jesus's sake, renew and increase in thee the gift of the Holy Spirit, thy strengthening in faith, thy growth in grace, they patience in suffering, and the blessed hope of everlasting life. Communion blessing. These words of truth were planted in my heart as a child. They return to me to consciously know and understand.

Night notes: "You can finish the writing." I see an image of several handwritten words and two white envelopes.

After meditation, there is white light (intelligence). Revelation: This is here now, the light is here now. Power is here now. I am empowered within my mind. How to do unselfishly (as a human)? "If it's good for you, it is good for me. Stand firm. Know

166

and feel truth. I am Christ Mind, one with all, simple, direct, peaceful, joyful, all power."

Patricia forsakes all others and clings to her beloved Self. Forsakes – to never return to the material state of consciousness that brought it about. God fulfills His Own Being as each one individually on earth. Seek only Spiritual realization (the Kingdom of God) in which God's grace is sufficiency in all things.

Grace, gift of God – only one gift – Himself. It unfolds in unthought of directions, unknown ways to us, forms we never dreamed would be part of our experience. Grace is individual. Patricia needed her judgment and fear revealed to her. She deserves a clear, unconditional mind to glorify her maker. She seeks only grace, and experiences it. God governs the body known as Patricia. She stands still, thinks no thoughts, and lets God's thoughts flow to, and permeate, her being. Spirit works in and through. Never for. Patricia surrenders all personal might and power. She can, of herself, do nothing. With God all things are possible.

In meditation: "Goodbye, dear." A physical woman speaking to me. No questions. "My God lives," I answered.

This is my continuous answer to all.

Night notes: Our faith is of God. God is our faith. I have no faith of myself. I ask in the name of God. My nerves scream like a baby who needs attention. What was the seeming error that brought this about? I believed there was an end to life; I feared being aborted. I am God, Life Eternal. Rejoice, Rejoice, Rejoice greatly. Felt and heard this. It came from within me.

I am awake and empowered by my Lord, by my very real Self. I feel a rejoicing from within. I am the glory of God. God is pleased with me. I am conscious of my connection, at one with Omnipotent Self, the power that raised Jesus Christ and me to the Father's Right Hand. I am one and the same. I am connected to the highest realm of thought, Christ Mind, enabling me to vision clearly and manifest consciously my Real Self, impersonal powers, and attributes. I thrill in communion, listening to your Voice, my own sweet, warm, tender Self within me. Your love surrounds and prepares the way, softening the conditions wherever I am. Rose fragrance rises to my awareness. Your warmth releasing the heart blooms of purity.

I am obeying the command to speak the Word in power. I felt the big toe of my left foot being grabbed. My entire left leg was being shaken. It was vibrating and shaking. My right leg then vibrated and shook. I felt tightening in my hips – they were firming and becoming secure. I *knew* this. I felt power going into them.

I am brought to awareness consciously of the power of life in my body, as one with it. What hinders me? A subconscious belief that I cannot help myself. I am afraid I can't help myself. I am a child being held down – sat on and tickled by my brother. I hate feeling helpless. I am unable to help myself. I wanted to kick my legs but my brother was sitting on them.

Catholic prayer: "Never let me offend you again. Grant that I may love you always and then do with me as you will."

Night notes: Image: A spider over my heart. Reveal to me consciously in understanding the cause of this muscle condition: TO CONSCIOUSLY KNOW THE FULLNESS OF MY POWER AS A SON OF GOD.

What was the belief in the past that needed correction and understanding? What was the core belief in the subconscious Race mind? Women are powerless over men. Each time we come into the world, each generation is evolving life to a higher level of Consciousness. Spirit is genderless. Seek ye first the Kingdom of Heaven, higher self, and consciously know my Will is One with my higher Self, the Will of God. Life is to give us the Kingdom. I accept my will to receive all knowledge, wisdom, power, happiness, health, and peace.

WE HAVE ALREADY BEEN GIVEN ALL IN OUR CREATION. KNOW THIS.

As I rest, I realize my ear is clear – heard a pop.

Night notes: "Nanny, your servant, John."

I open to the highest realm of thought, Soul, Mind, and Body to receive God's perfect image as I am envisioned or conceived in God's mind and heart. I ask what I will, for the asking is given me. I am in *your* image. I am your image. A fragrance comes – sulfur. Remembering. I see energy patterns: a foggy light – clear away space to receive. A tender melting of tears. I forever remember You, feel you, know you in every fiber of my being. Knowing in Spirit is as feeling in senses translated to mind of human being. Unspeakable experience – words cannot describe. It is forever in me, all of us. Remember.

Eye of Horus – dot of light – intelligence. Light is coming. In this world, it takes time to receive and feel, KNOW.

Night notes: Vision experience: Sophia comes to my body. I embrace her. "My back hurts." I feel and hear the spine straighten. "Do you want me to work on it?" "Mother isn't feeling well. She needs me tonight."[54] Remember feeling well – empowered. Bring it to mind.

Meditation: Begotten of the Father. I am image and likeness of God. I am in the mind of God. I am mind of God. I am Mary, womb of God. I am feminine aspect, tender and receiving. Handmaiden of the Lord. I bring forth manifestation of God in flesh. Remember feeling gentle strength of power, being enabled.

Remember me. I remember you, Lord. I know you intimately. Female voice: "I will click to it." I immediately receive image which I am in God's Mind. The Ethiopian asked, received word, and immediately gave it forth, empowered by it.[55] Express memory which is feeling one with God. Your way is wonderful, Lord. How do I do this? Mind is my servant. I do nothing. Behold, receive. IT IS SO. Accept.

Realize – in intellect this *must be true.* God's will for me and my will for my Self. I accept God's vision of me. "Your servant, John." The realization of truth came to conscious mind from Christ Mind. Father Rodrigo (priest at my church parish) anointed me. I

---

[54] Night is a time of darkness of the intellect. The light of Christ, understanding, is needed.

[55] Acts 8:32–39.

accepted this. I am anointed one. I am consecrated to God. Confirmed truth.

Night notes: I raised a shade a third of the way up and light entered. I opened to more light and understanding, which is power – understanding self. I saw myself running up and down my stairs, fast forward motion time. When I got up and walked, I felt a slight pain. I also felt empowered in movement. I sang powerfully: Holy, holy, holy. Glory to God.

Night notes: "Birthday of a King," a song we sang in junior choir at church, sang out of me spontaneously, without thought. Image of a One-eyed owl. Source is impersonal God. (Source of all life is God. God is Source.)

Awakened twice by movement similar to a disc slipping but without pain. Powerful movement within my hip. No fear.

April 20, Easter morning

I FELT HANDS RUN SLOWLY DOWN MY BACK, BRINGING TINGLING AND LIFE. "I AM COME FOR YOU. REMEMBER, I AM WITH YOU ALWAYS, FOREVER. USE ME. LIVE ME IN MIND AND HEART. I AM LIFE ETERNAL. I AM WORD OF LIFE TO YOU. LET ME LIVE IN YOU. ALLOW ME TO FULFILL MY PROMISE IN YOU. I WILL. ASK WHAT YOU WILL. IT WILL BE DONE. BELIEVE IN ME." I WILL. AMEN.

Night notes: "Natural is always happening." I stand corrected. Holy Spirit is corrector. Give me your thought. I felt softening and deep tenderness within.

"I AM ALL. I, only, live in you. I, only, am Life. Listen to me. I love you. You are my child. Feel my Love. My Love is all. I am Love. I AM YOU. You are Love. Love Lives you. This Love is your Life, your Self.

Yes, I have come for you. Yes, I am here for you. I AM Love Living in Love. You are Love Living in me. Only Love *IS*. Only God *IS*." I see a large sphere of pink energy in my mind. I felt the correction in my sacrum. I felt a shift, realized in mind and body. I Stand corrected. I AM corrected. I AM correction. Thank you, love.

IN REALITY, LOVE IS ALL.

Readings and other resources that have influenced Patricia throughout her life:

Spiritual Influences:

- Mother, who had a near-death experience at age thirteen and other mystical occurrences throughout her life, several of which I was a part. These experiences are not recorded here. Her faith in God is alive.

- St. John's Evangelical Lutheran Church, Rev. Russell S. Gaenzle, D.D.

- Sir David R. Hawkins, M.D., Ph.D. – Various books and lecture study group.

- Peg Haraske – Spiritual teacher and friend.

Books:

- *A Course in Miracles: Combined Volume*, by Foundation for Inner Peace

- *A Search for God, Books I & II*, by Edgar Cayce and Edgar Cayce Study Group Association for Research and Enlightenment

- *Autobiography of a Yogi*, by Paramahansa Yogananda

- *Bhagavad–Gita: The Song of God*, translated by Swami Prabhavananda and Christopher Isherwood

- *Cosmic Consciousness: A Study in the Evolution of the Human Mind*, by Richard Maurice Bucke

- *Everyman's Search, Everyman's Mission, Everyman's Goal*, by Rebecca Beard

- *How to Know God: The Yoga Aphorisms of Patanjali*, translated by Swami Prabhavananda and Christopher Isherwood

- *Mysticism: A Study in the Nature and Development of Spiritual Consciousness*, by Evelyn Underhill

- *Psychological Commentaries on the Teaching of Gurdjieff and Ouspensky*, by Maurice Nicoll

- *Tertium Organum*, by P.D. Ouspensky

- The Bible

- *The Celebrated 14th Century Mystic and Scholastic Meister Eckhart*, translated by Raymond B. Blakney

- *The Cloud of Unknowing*, edited by Robert Baldick and Betty Radice

- *The Healing Light*, by Agnes Sanford

- *The I Ching or Book of Changes*, translated by Richard Wilhelm and Cary F. Baynes

- *The Infinite Way*, by Joel S. Goldsmith

- *The Practice of the Presence of God,* by Brother Lawrence

- *The Science of Mind,* by Ernest Holmes

- *Three Magic Words,* by U.S. Andersen

Acknowledgements

Gratitude to my daughter Donna, whose elegant and tender heart You opened to receive and transcribe in its purity Your message of love.

Kudos to grandson James whose computer savviness and great love and patience brought this manuscript to fruition and Sophia's song to life.

To Stephanie J. Beavers – the perfect editor for this manuscript. Your skillful and bold presentation of the typical reader's need to understand this material, brought to light the clear, simple unalterable nugget of truth that needs no embellishment. It stands on its own eternally in unspeakable splendor. You are a gift.

Made in the USA
Lexington, KY
04 November 2019